Contents

Co-operation or Competition? Defence Procurement Options for the 1990s

INTRODUCTION

Of making many books (and pamphlets and articles) on the subject of conventional weapons procurement policy, there is seemingly no end. For example, it has already been addressed, in varying degrees of depth, in five Adelphi Papers, and much other material has been published in the 20–25 years during which it has been a matter of serious debate and concern.

The reason for this is that the combined equipment expenditure of the Alliance nations is vast. The European nations alone planned to spend some $43 bn[1] on new equipment in 1989. The United Kingdom was not untypical of the leading NATO nations in planning to spend 43% of its defence budget on equipment in 1988–9. At some $15 bn, this was more than double the total budgets of all but four of the UK's Departments of State.[2] With sums as large as this at stake, defence planners and politicians do not lack advice on what the money should be used to buy and how it should be spent. Procurement options range from purchasing everything possible from indigenous industry, through various forms of licensed or co-production, to international collaboration (defined here as inter-government agreement to procure equipment produced jointly by their national industries to meet a joint military requirement), and, finally, international competition. Of these, until very recently, the majority of European countries thought that, for major buys demanding 'leading edge' technology, sharing costs through government-inspired and managed collaborative procurement was the best means of affording the next generation of equipment. Any imperfections and inefficiencies associated with collaborative projects – and the scale of these inefficiencies is a matter of keen contention – would have to be swallowed. The alternative solution to the problem of affordability – lowering costs through open international competition in a free market, which need not exclude co-operation between firms – was solemnly averred to be 'politically impossible'.

The factors which prompted collaboration, first acting as catalysts in the 1960s and early 1970s, continue to operate. For example, in an Adelphi Paper published in 1975,[3] Roger Facer drew attention to the spiralling unit costs of defence equipment, which led to procurement budgets being dominated by a handful of expensive, mainly aerospace, projects. The technological sophistication of these projects meant that, in turn, a higher proportion of the budget had to go on support, leaving less for the next generation of equipment. He also pointed out, that in a period of *détente*, defence budgets and equipment markets were being constrained. This analysis remains fundamentally unaltered.

When action was needed to relieve the problem there were obvious attractions in collaboration. The financial benefits of shared development expenditure – avoidance of duplication and the achievement of longer production runs – were judged to outweigh the compromises in requirements which collaboration demands, and the higher overall costs which these partnerships attract. The possibility of this new arrangement being seen as closing sectors of the European arms market to American industry would have to be faced. For two decades, therefore, equipment collaboration has featured in the procurement policies of the major European nations.

Despite the interest in collaboration over this period, nations still act independently to procure the majority of their equipment. Moreover, the factors which led countries to pioneer European collaboration as a solution to the problem of affordability have been given an altered perspective with experience and the passage of time. A new and more relaxed spirit is abroad. Edward Heath, writing recently about the progress of European unity, has commented that 'In time there will come a common defence and procurement policy with a common foreign policy as its basis'[4] – which implies a common internal European market in arms.

Changing attitudes

There is already considerable evidence that procurement policies are being modified and the established procurement methods challenged. For example, Jacques Chevallier, until 1989 the French National Armaments Director, although eschewing 'unbridled liberalism', has called for a lowering of protectionist barriers, and observed, in parallel, that collaboration at all costs is not necessarily the answer. Even when it is, a competitive element is essential.[5] Further evidence is provided by the UK government's response to an observation from its House of Commons Defence Committee. The text is revealing:

> The government does not regard international collaboration as an end in itself, but as a means of securing value for money in appropriate circumstances . . . This [international procurement] strategy, which the government is encouraging our allies to share, includes a more open defence market and a greater willingness for nations to buy each other's equipment off the shelf.[6]

What has changed, of course, is governments' fairly recent, and by no means universal, adoption of competition as the most effective means of achieving 'value for money' when buying new equipment, even

4

though tests of 'value' remain imperfectly articulated and have yet to be made the subject of convincing demonstrations. Moreover, international collaboration and competition continue to be ridden in tandem despite the incompatibility that exists between them.

There are those, including the United Kingdom government, who claim not to find the twin objectives of collaboration and competition in Europe incompatible.[7] This study will assess whether riding competition and government-to-government collaboration in harness has to or can continue, whether it is likely to result in value for money and whether it is too hazardous, either to the security of Alliance nations, or to their economic prosperity, to allow the market a greater say in arms procurement. For change is in the air. The pressure of the European Commission's open market policy in public procurement is gradually, and perhaps inevitably, eroding the barriers against a truly free arms market in Europe. A case can be made for national governments not to waste their energies in seeking to stem this development but to build on it to increase industrial efficiency at home and competitiveness abroad; nevertheless real or imagined political problems surrounding the defence industries cannot be ignored. As Geoffrey Howe, commenting on the political appeal of domestic defence procurement when UK Foreign Secretary, has said:

> It's much less easy to explain why the non-national option may represent in the long run better value for money and more long-term assurance of technical survival.[8]

It is legitimate, however, to ask why this is so and whether politicians themselves contribute to or even, on occasion, fan public anxiety over the industrial component of national security.

There is no doubt that such concerns are in part warranted. Massive international collaborative projects have done little to solve the European defence industries' problems of excess capacity and fragmentation. There is, therefore, a need to search for alternative and more economically efficient forms of co-operation which might be evolved to supersede the early European and transatlantic models: new models which might sit more easily with a parallel drive to obtain value for money from competition. For the present approach to collaboration and, to a degree, such competition as there is within Europe at prime contractor level, is substantially impaired (to an extent explored later in this Paper) by a declared and generally rigid government adherence to the principle of *juste retour* (a fair economic and technical return on each partner's contribution to the collaboration). This principle is coupled with an equally industrially questionable commitment to give countries with 'less developed defence industries' (LDDI) work which they would be unlikely to win in open competition. The central question here is whether or not the economic inefficiency this involves is outweighed by a contribution to Alliance cohesion. It is both significant and regrettable that Independent European Programme

Group (IEPG) ministers, in announcing in November 1988 the adoption of an Action Plan to open their defence contracts to competitive bidding, with value for money as the guiding principle – in theory a step forward of the first significance – were constrained to accept both that cross-border competitiveness depended on countries obtaining a fair return over an acceptable period of time, and that LDDI nations should be assisted.[9]

Proponents of the scheme and pragmatists would say in its defence that an agreement of this kind was the best that could be negotiated. Incremental progress is all that can be expected when so much is at stake. Just how much progress towards a more efficient system of arms procurement the Action Plan represents, remains to be seen. It has yet to be implemented. But with a new direction in prospect, this seems an appropriate time to ask whether the continuance of a policy of allocating work to existing European defence companies, which have serious problems of over-capacity, whilst simultaneously encouraging the creation of additional capacity, is inevitable. Is the perpetuation of the goal of maximum self-sufficiency in arms, in which international collaboration plays a part, any longer realistic, achievable and affordable?

Of course it is the duty of governments to take every necessary action they can to preserve the security of the state. If they judge it necessary for this purpose to maintain a fully capable aerospace or shipbuilding industry, or any other aspect of a national defence industrial base (DIB), there should therefore be no complaints. In fact, however, the military case for self-sufficiency in today's world is not a powerful one. The list of truly vital capabilities is short, and in any case, changes over time. Moreover, even the most advanced manufacturers have a significant and growing reliance on the US and Japan as sources of components and technology. This, taken together with substantial foreign investment in defence companies, means that Alliance governments are in practice unable to opt for total self-sufficiency, even if they are so inclined. The technical and economic cases for maintaining national capabilities are also by no means impregnable. If self-sufficiency were judged to be of supreme importance we would not expect to find economically-developed states apparently willing to rely on foreign arms suppliers, nor content to leave their security to an alliance. Governments' propensities over the years to preserve extensive national defence industrial capabilities are therefore surprising and not easy to explain.

Sovereignty

Of course, it could be claimed that, while a nation may choose not to create an indigenous arms industry, it is quite another matter to give one up, or to risk its loss by exposing the companies involved to free competition. Public reaction would be negative: it could even be argued that sovereignty would be at stake.

However, it is doubtful whether the somewhat fustian notion of sovereignty is a matter of deep day-to-day popular and therefore political concern. In economically-advanced countries, governments and the governed share a common concern to see that there is sufficient standing military force available to them to prevail in a conflict. It is more doubtful whether today's taxpayers feel equally strongly about the origin of the equipment used by that force. To some degree, feelings on the point are simply dormant, for effective lobbying can rouse them, but if national self-sufficiency in arms becomes a totem, it can be an expensive one to maintain. It is also an odd one when the sovereignty so often paraded as the reason for maintaining national arms capabilities has, in Europe, in part been surrendered through signature of the Treaty of Rome. The governments signing that Treaty pooled certain aspects of their sovereignty for the common good of the European Community (EC), just as most of them pool the bulk of their defence resources through their commitments to the North Atlantic Alliance.

Socially, the creation of the EC has meant that more and more people, whether consciously or not, are adopting the dual nationality of 'European' alongside that of the country of their birth. Small wonder, when younger people can only remember relying for their security on collective defence arrangements which came into being in 1949. A 'British Lifestyle' survey, published early in 1989, revealed that 68% of the insular Britons of continental European legend favoured the concept of a United States of Europe, provided the UK still made its own decisions, and 38% said they already regarded themselves as European as well as British. Among 'opinion formers' support was even stronger, a majority seeing themselves as Europeans and 72% favouring a United States of Europe.[10] Economically, the countries of Europe and the world are becoming more interdependent and the defence industries themselves more international. But there remains a need for each country to be able to take independent sovereign action if necessary. Is that right threatened if the defence industries are unprotected?

The need for readjustment
The capability to act alone militarily remains a good but, in an economically interdependent world, not a sufficient reason for governments to nurture their defence industries. Why, then, are they preserved? The answer usually given is that the DIB creates and sustains jobs and brings less easily quantified technological and economic benefits. However, the importance of defence jobs and technology in social and economic terms is open to a variety of interpretations. What is not in dispute is that governments have been reluctant to come to terms with the need for the structural readjustment that an opening of the market would bring.

Trevor Taylor recorded his impressions of the problem in a book published seven years ago:

> governments feel paralysed by the risk, complexity and importance of negotiations on integrating European defence industries . . . it would force government machines to make hard decisions on which sectors need to be protected and promoted and which abandoned.[11]

Sovereignty, he concluded, was not a significant consideration and 'muddling through' would remain the order of the day. So it has proved. Creating a flow of equipment projects to sustain national industries remains a key driver of procurement decisions. The structure of major new procurements like the European Fighter Aircraft (EFA), for all the effort that has been made to maximize the scope for competition in the project, still reflects the principle of *juste retour*.

Meanwhile, procurement budgets, for a variety of well-understood reasons, first in the US and now in Europe, are being squeezed harder than overall defence budgets, which are themselves under pressure and in some countries declining in real terms. For example, in November 1989 the US Defense Secretary announced that he was looking for cuts in defence spending of $10–15 bn in the fiscal year beginning in October 1990, and cuts in planned expenditure of up to $180 bn over the next three years. This could be equivalent to a real cut of $50 bn and, inevitably, much of it will fall on equipment. Giving the International Institute for Strategic Studies' Alastair Buchan Memorial Lecture in November 1988, NATO's Secretary General, Manfred Wörner, said 'The Alliance's task is to legitimise its continued defence efforts at a time when the public perception is that a robust defence policy is less than necessary'. Within three weeks Mikhail Gorbachev announced dramatic unilateral reductions in Soviet forces and other Eastern bloc countries followed suit. Little more than a year later the Warsaw Pact had ceased to be a coherent military threat and an ambitious timescale had been set for the conclusion of a treaty reducing Conventional Forces in Europe (CFE). It is impossible yet to predict what the effect of these developments on defence budgets will be but one thing is already certain: there will be public pressure for cuts in defence spending, the much advertised 'peace dividend'.

If there is to be no extra money for defence and no increase in equipment budgets, we should look at whether there are other ways and means of securing real value for money in defence procurement. Such means might include the creation of a more open market, and resolution of the debate about what the role of governments should be in relation to the defence industries.

Scope
Taking as an underpinning assumption the belief that the emerging system of international relations in Europe will continue to entail a security role for the Atlantic Alliance and be largely centred on a vigor-

ous European Community, this Paper begins by looking at how equipment requirements are laid down now and have been in the past, both nationally and internationally within NATO. It traces the efforts to rationalize, harmonize and integrate them and explains the reasons for the disappointing progress that has been made. There have been failures of institutions and failures of planning systems.

Chapter 2 assesses the potential contribution that the IEPG Action Plan will make towards a better order, and then examines the defence industries in the US and Europe, their current and future state of health and their abilities to meet military demands. It argues that many sectors of these industries are ill-prepared to cope with the harsh winds of competition, currently mere zephyrs, which will be fanned to gale force in the areas of depression caused by Alliance-wide equipment budget cuts.

Chapter 3 looks at how current and past procurement practice has contributed to this situation and identifies the need for more radical change than that which has so far been contemplated. In particular it suggests that a freer market than the IEPG envisages, with the cost savings it should bring, is the only affordable solution to universal budgetary pressures.

Chapter 4 focuses on factors which are prompting the changes that are needed, and the implications for the defence industries on both sides of the Atlantic of the advent of an internal market in Europe in 1992. The countervailing forces which will continue to hinder progress are also analysed.

The study concludes that too little progress is being made too slowly, and that, rather than believing that a workable way forward in defence procurement has been found, Western European and North American nations should allow market forces to bring about radical restructuring. If they do not, value for money will remain a chimera.

I. PROCUREMENT PLANNING

A nation's defence equipment plan is no less important and serious than any other element of its military preparedness. Having the right equipment available to meet the full spectrum of military needs, in the right quantities, in the right place and at the right time, and, increasingly, at the right price, is of vital concern to commanders.

Like war itself, however, equipment planning is too important to be left to the generals. Given the historic preference of the larger European nations and the US for a high degree of self-sufficiency in arms supply, and a consequential need to maintain substantial industrial capacity, it is inevitable that there are many fingers in the equipment decision-making pie. A host of factors have to be taken into account, and many pressures have either to be resisted or responded to. This makes the decision-making process, even within one nation, labyrinthine and protracted. In collaborative projects, involving several countries, these complexities and delays are compounded. But although collaborative projects absorb increasing proportions of individual service equipment budgets, there are still only a few of them. After 25 years or more of collaborative ventures, as of early 1990 the UK has only four out of 39 major projects that are the subject of inter-government collaborative agreements.[1] Moreover, 75% of the UK's equipment expenditure is with its national industry. If the work generated by collaborative projects is included, this figure rises to 90%. France, Germany and the US also have high levels of self-sufficiency which require and sustain national defence industries with the capacity to design, develop and produce equipment and to support it in service.

Table 1: Indigenous equipment expenditure by value
(including indigenous element of collaborative ventures)

		%
France	$\approx$	95
Germany	$\approx$	70
UK	$\approx$	90
US	$\approx$	98

National decision-making
Although the overt or covert protection of national defence industries in the cause of military self-sufficiency is common amongst the major nations of the Alliance, there are some differences of philosophy and practice. Traditionally, the US, with its sustained high level of equipment expenditure, has given contractors a great deal of programme management responsibility. The European nations, on the other hand, have operated cautious approval procedures designed to minimize technical and financial risk through rigid control by ministers and

officials, although this approach is now being eased to give greater responsibility to contractors, on the US model.

Whatever system is adopted, the common aim is to obtain equipment which works, at a given time and at a given cost. This is not as simple as it sounds. The development period for a complex project can last ten years, while completing the planned production run can take a further five to ten. The equipment may then have an in-service life of 20 years or more. During this period the operational threat that it is designed to meet can, and does, change. Hence the need for much of military equipment Research and Development (R&D) to operate at the leading edge of new technology, and for 'mid-life updates' for equipments which tend to be obsolescent the day they enter service because of their long development timescales.

There are four basic reasons why new equipment is needed, although clear lines cannot always be drawn between them and mixed motives often apply. These are:

– The development of new military concepts or strategies demanding new or enhanced capabilities.
– Intelligence assessments of future or altered military threats.
– The development of new technology, either by government or industry, offering new capabilities of significant military utility (in the context of national or alliance strategic needs).
– The need to replace existing equipment which is no longer reliable or cannot be maintained.

The overlap between these motivating forces in terms of the generation of R&D programmes is obvious. The US Strategic Defense Initiative is a particularly prominent case in point. The gestation period during which one or more of these factors becomes sufficiently powerful to give rise to a new equipment requirement is highly variable, ranging from the very long to the very short. The process of generating new needs is triggered by both episodic and cyclic events.

Throughout the R&D phase the proposed equipment will have been subject to scrutiny, testing and questioning from a wide range of sources. Political, financial, export sales, employment, industrial policy and military advisers will all have had their say. In addition, the firms with contracts at stake will have done their own lobbying. Reaching a decision on whether a project should live or die is therefore a difficult, arduous and not always rational process. Even the adoption of 'commercial' disciplines, now increasingly in vogue in the major spending countries of the Alliance, does not free decisions on major items of public expenditure from other constraints.

Alliance equipment planning – the elusive ideal
Whatever the imperfections associated with these national processes, they are at least immediately directed towards the production of effective military hardware, to time and to cost. The same cannot yet be

said of the supranational NATO-wide equipment planning arrangements currently in effect. For it is at the planning level that NATO arms co-ordination stops. Such translation of multinational planning into military hardware as there has been, has to date been almost exclusively achieved through national government initiatives. If these have become 'NATO' projects, it is because Brussels has adopted them rather than created them. The workings of the many institutions, both formally within the NATO ambit and outside it, have so far served only further to complicate an already baroque project decision-making process. However, urgent, even dramatic, steps are being taken to improve matters.

Improvement is long overdue. The European Defence Community, proposed in the early 1950s, had it succeeded, was to have incorporated a centralized procurement system. Equipment was to have been planned and bought collectively. The Defence Community's writ would also have run to the supply side, which would have led to the reshaping and rationalization of continental Europe's defence industries. In essence, what was envisaged was a common European defence market. This remarkably far-sighted concept was not translated into action.

Although the opportunity to act collectively in matters of defence had been lost, economic co-operation in Europe flourished. The EEC was established in 1958, paving the way for the liberalization of trade and the eventual removal of tariff and trade barriers. Military equipment, however, was excluded from the common market features of the Community, no doubt to avoid jeopardizing agreement to the Treaty of Rome through arousing opposition in a sensitive area. This left NATO as the chief international forum for co-ordinating the procurement of standardized, or at least interoperable, defence equipment.

The objective of commonality was not new. A Military Production and Supply Board, concerned with promoting standardization and improving procurement methods, had been set up in NATO in 1949. By 1950 it had become the Defence Production Board. Organizational change continued, at times at a quite bewildering rate, but efforts to create an effective weapons-planning machinery made little real progress in the face of nations' continuing refusal to establish a central procurement agency with common funding and some autonomy. Today, organizational change and the creation of new planning systems continues at a brisk pace, but the goal of co-operation remains largely elusive. At the heart of the problem lies the fact that however sophisticated the planning machinery, it cannot overcome a situation in which people are basically unwilling to work together. The history of the NATO Basic Military Requirements (NBMR) procedure, adopted in 1959, helps to explain why.

The NBMR procedure stemmed from the realization that although nations seemed determined to continue to procure their weapons independently, this should not prevent military requirements from being co-ordinated. Under the NBMR system, both national and NATO staff could make recommendations. If these received collective support they would be accepted by the Military Committee as NATO requirements. Thereafter, common development and production was to be arranged by the nations procuring the equipment. And therein lay the rub. Although the military side of NATO could agree on requirements, national policies ruled when it came to financial and industrial concerns. Precisely the same situation exists today. The outcome was that despite agreement on 49 NBMRs during the seven-year life of the system, seven were procured from existing national stocks and no weapons were developed specifically to meet an NBMR. The collective will to make the system work was lacking and the arrangements were abandoned in 1966.

CNAD

Undaunted, the NATO nations, believing limited co-operation to be preferable to none, established, in the late 1960s, a body of senior officials known as the Conference of National Armaments Directors (CNAD). This institution, which ranks alongside NATO's Military Committee (MC), is still in existence. Within the Alliance, the CNAD and the MC are the organizations primarily concerned with issues of interoperability and collaboration. However, the NBMR's objective of establishing NATO-wide requirements has been replaced by a more modest one. The CNAD provides a mechanism by means of which any two or more countries agreeing a common requirement, and establishing a collaborative development and production plan, can bring the project under the NATO umbrella. This, however, from a national viewpoint, is not always an unmixed blessing.

CNAD has six Main Groups, representing each nation's armed services, specialist interests and defence industries. The working and study groups flowing from the Main Groups address individual opportunities for collective acquisition, in terms of requirements and timescales. Some major new NATO projects were conceived as a consequence, although not all of these have survived to come to fruition (the most recent failure being the 1989–90 collapse of the eight-nation NATO Frigate Replacement (NFR–90) programme).

CNAD's most valuable contribution has been its untiring commitment to achieving within the Alliance an acceptance that working from identified operational deficiencies towards harmonized equipment solutions should be the rule rather than the exception. In particular it has, in part, overcome the deficiencies of NATO's well-intentioned, but largely ineffective, Consolidated National Defence Equipment Schedule (CNDES). The aim of the CNDES is to ensure that all Alliance nations are aware of each other's replacement plans. Twenty-year equipment replacement plans are sought, collated, examined for their interoperability and collaborative potential and fed back. It is a useful process but does not, of itself, establish the impetus to collaborate. Moreover, the programmes scheduled are frequently too far advanced easily to be turned into co-operative ventures. Fruitful collaboration starts upstream of the point at which equipment programmes are codified; before the point at which the operational requirement is settled. The recognition of this fact has spawned yet more Alliance-wide planning systems and procedures.

Periodic Armaments Planning System (PAPS)
Chief amongst these, until recently, was PAPS, introduced in 1981. The system's point of departure is a military requirement expressed as a 'mission need' – a statement of quantitative or qualitative operational deficiency that cannot be satisfactorily solved with existing or planned forces and/or equipment. By laying down this pivotal principle, it was hoped that the military would resist the siren call of new technology for its own sake.

The statements of mission need can be generated by both national and NATO staffs. CNAD bodies then subject them to detailed examination, with the aim of converting them, after study of their feasibility, into a full NATO staff requirement which will be satisfied by some form of co-operative venture; a venture which other nations can join if they discover that they have the same requirement, even though they were not initially involved.

The probability of success of such a system is, of course, crucially dependent on international agreement to the mission need itself. But, just as in the NBMR system, NATO can only act as a facilitator in creating a supportive environment and bureaucracy in which 'togetherness' can prosper. Because NATO is not a supranational organization with the power to direct national governments, it has no option but to step aside once national decisions come to be made on how individual forces are to be equipped. Feeding a mission need into PAPS does not, of itself, ensure that there will be a common solution to the requirement it describes.

Although PAPS has been in operation for some eight years and much effort has been spent on its introduction and operation, its record of achievement in terms of getting equipment into production on a co-operative basis has been poor. Perhaps too much has been expected of it too soon. The process of harmonizing specifications is painfully slow. It may therefore be some years before PAPS can be fairly assessed. However, there does not appear to be any very marked political willingness to make it work. Indeed, in recognition of the fact that PAPS is unlikely ever to impose Alliance-wide order on the introduction of new equipment, a trial of yet another system is now under way.

Conventional Armaments Planning System (CAPS)
The basic idea of the CAPS scheme is that the Alliance keeps nations better informed of its commanders' equipment goals, and nations respond by keeping the Alliance informed about their own armaments

plans. Obviously, the aim is to ensure that as far as possible the armaments goals of NATO's major military commanders are reflected in the equipment plans of the individual nations. And, as with PAPS, the new system will seek, early in the planning process, to identify opportunities for co-operative development and production.

CAPS has now completed a two-year trial which has been judged successful and is to be extended. It is the most vigorous attempt yet made within NATO to make the equipment needs of the Alliance and its members one and the same. If it leads to the creation of a conventional armaments plan that is adopted and adhered to, it will have made a major contribution to the strength of the Alliance. Most notably, the prospects for national co-operation in equipment procurement will, in theory, have been transformed, since requirements will have already been harmonized through national agreement to a NATO armaments goal.

But it would be a mistake to expect too much of CAPS, at least in the short term. Its limitations are essentially those of PAPS. Results, even in terms of harmonized requirements, will be slow in coming because the price of adherence to the lofty principles of equipment rationalization in terms of the abandonment of national decision-making remains too high. Nations can only be persuaded, not coerced, to buy the equipment the Alliance would like them to have. Additionally, much will depend on whether the United States is enthusiastic about CAPS. Present indications are that it is not. The US seems to favour a more pragmatic approach, preferring to bring nations together through joining them in multilateral and bilateral projects funded under the Roth–Glenn–Nunn Amendment to the FY 1986 US defence budget, which earmarked an annual $100–150 m for NATO collaborative projects rooted in established needs. Not even NATO itself seems to be counting on success. The Defence Planning Committee has said that CAPS '*might* assist in providing a necessary link between military requirements defined for the future and armaments planning in the long term' (author's emphasis).[2]

There is no doubt that such a link is necessary. One of the reasons why it has not yet been successfully established is the profusion of bodies involved in armaments planning. Thus, within a purely European context, the functions of NATO's planning systems are largely duplicated by the non-NATO Independent European Programme Group.

The Independent European Programme Group (IEPG)
The IEPG was formed in 1976. It consists of the European nations integrated in the NATO military structure, together with France. Indeed, the creation of this further institution, formally outside the Alliance, was in response to a need to create a non-NATO European forum to promote, facilitate and monitor armaments co-operation, in which France could participate. While one of its progenitors, the EUROGROUP, which was founded in 1968, includes Sub-Groups

concerned with long-term planning and with armaments procurement, and in 1970 put together the five-year European Defence Improvement Programme (EDIP), France's non-participation significantly limited the organization's utility, and its armament procurement activities have virtually ceased since the IEPG was established.

The functions performed by the IEPG parallel those of the other planning schemes. It collects information on nations' long-term equipment plans with a view to identifying opportunities for collaboration. Also on the Group's agenda is the reverse process of generating specific proposals which might in due course be launched as European collaborative ventures.

From its inception until 1984 the IEPG was largely ineffective, isolated from the real world of procurement planning, because there was a lack of political determination to make the organization achieve its potential. There were continuing fears that the United States might be alarmed to the point of action by a serious display of European unity. And there were reciprocal fears within Europe. From the point of view of countries with established arms industries there was no sense in promoting fresh competition from the smaller European nations – a view which still persists. The smaller nations, on the other hand, did not yet feel that their industries were sufficiently strong to play in a big league. They preferred to continue with a system of ordering based on government protection. The IEPG therefore effectively achieved nothing.

However, in 1984, the UK's Defence Secretary of the day, Michael Heseltine, was beginning vigorously to promote to his European colleagues his enthusiasm for European defence co-operation which, he claimed, would go hand in hand with the rationalization of European defence industries. One of the consequences was an agreement in November 1984 that the IEPG should, for the first time, meet at ministerial level on an *ad hoc* basis. The idea was that under firm political direction the IEPG would become more positive and innovative. To some degree the idea has worked. In the intervening years the Group has agreed 15 European Staff Targets, of varying provenance. Useful work has also been done on harmonizing operational requirements and procurement timescales, subject to ministerial overview. Upstream, pre-competitive technological collaboration has also been initiated, through the creation of Co-operative Technology Projects. Finally, from the beginning of 1989, the Group's activities were restructured to make them more effective, and a permanent secretariat set up (in Lisbon).

At the working level, the IEPG operates with 'panels' staffed by national officials, who combine their work for the Group with other roles in their national defence ministries. On the one hand, however, this arrangement is cost- and resource-effective, on the other it means that panel members find it hard to depart from their national 'party line' when the inevitable compromises have to be made in the cause of harmonizing requirements. In an effort to minimize this problem a

16

single IEPG panel has now been created to deal with both the harmonization of operational requirements and the launching of collaborative ventures. It will therefore be more obvious to ministers and to National Armaments Directors (NADs) when military inflexibility on a requirement is hindering the inception of a collaborative project. The job of the panel is to agree requirements, identify 'goers' – industrially, politically and financially – and to drive them to an industrialization phase. A second panel, created in 1989, now concentrates on research and Co-operative Technology Projects. A third is charged with considering the implications of the creation of a more open European market in arms, and advising on the consequences of the establishment in Europe by 1992 of open public procurement arrangements, even though items used solely for military purposes are at present excluded from such arrangements. It will also examine the scope for 'off-the-shelf' arms purchases by IEPG nations.

Table 2: Extant multinational planning systems

System	Purpose	Assessment
Conference of National Armaments Directors (CNAD)	Promotion of requirement harmonization	Long-established; bureaucratic; not supranational; modest but growing success
Consolidated National Defence Equipment Schedule (CNDES)	Information feedback	Too late to be effective
Periodic Armaments Planning System (PAPS)	Creating harmonized mission needs	Poor track record; lacks US backing; not supranational
Conventional Armaments Planning System (CAPS)	Linking NATO armaments goals with long-term national plans	Successfully trialled; not supranational; unlikely to make major short-term impact
Independent European Programme Group (IEPG)	Promoting European collaboration	Recently revitalized and reorganized; includes France; not supranational; duplicates CNAD for European nations; modest progress; no concrete achievement

To date, however, the revitalized IEPG has not succeeded in moving a single project into an industrialization phase. The explanation for the IEPG's failure to deliver lies in the fact that, like its sister bodies, it has no institutionalized role to play in national armaments planning. Nonetheless, it does play a useful part in obliging equipment planners to identify co-operative opportunities.

Alliance planning systems are summarized in Table 2.

The Vredeling Report

One piece of work by the IEPG has been of particular significance. In 1984, ministers directed that there should be a study of the means by which the competitiveness of Europe's defence industries could be increased. The study was to focus on the rationalization of the supply side, including research and future large investment. The following year, agreement was reached to expand the study to include all aspects of the defence industries, including national procurement policies.

The study was conducted by ten independent 'wise men', experienced in procurement matters, under the chairmanship of the former Dutch Defence Minister, Henk Vredeling. Their comprehensive, two-volume report, 'Towards a Stronger Europe', which included the results of specially commissioned work on the technological threat facing Europe, was presented to NADs at the beginning of 1987.

The Report calls for nationalistic procurement policies to be abandoned and a series of steps to be taken to create, in time, an open European armaments market. The authors of the Report saw this objective as being underpinned by governments formally agreeing that:

a) they are prepared to adopt a policy of competition across Europe;
b) they will not distort the market directly or indirectly.

Unhappily, in two respects, these principles are undermined rather than underpinned, in the small print of the study's recommendations. Governments were never required to adopt these two principles.

Firstly, the Report makes 'more clarity and structure in the arrangements for *juste retour*' an essential prerequisite for the achievement of an open market. In practice, a 'fair return' means that nations expect to get back in work the equivalent of what they put in in money – and preferably more! Such a system is clearly inimical to competition. It also distorts the market. There appears to be some tacit recognition in the Report that this is so because it is suggested that, rather than have *juste retour* organized within a single project, as it is at present, the return should be spread over several projects and over a longer period. This minimizes, but unfortunately does not eliminate, the inefficiencies associated with *juste retour*.

The second weakness in the Report is the special pleading it contains on behalf of the less developed defence industry (LDDI) nations – Greece, Turkey and Portugal. The proposal is made that the stronger nations of Europe should help these nations to strengthen their technological bases and develop their defence industries. What is envisaged is the allocation of suitable high technology work to LDDI nations on a

18

case-by-case basis, though it did not address the cost implications of doing so.

The argument for this is said in the Report to be essentially political; it was thought vital to the economic, social and industrial integration of Europe. However, apart from the possibility of the LDDI nations seeking to satisfy their hunger for technology outside Europe, it is not clear quite why building up their defence industries should be so vital to European integration. There are many other developments which would have greater symbolic and practical significance.

The notion of support for LDDI nations is not new, and the larger nations periodically express support for it, but without a great deal of practical result. Thus NATO's Defence Planning Committee stated, at the end of 1988, 'Current extensive defence efforts by the LDDI countries are less effective than they could be by virtue of the lack of appropriate Allied assistance'.[3]

The reasons for this are not hard to find. Nations do not wish actively to assist in the creation of new industrial competition. The governments of the major European nations either seek to protect and promote their own defence contractors or they are the willing victims of powerful industrial lobbies which work to the same ends. Either way, there is little economic sense in adding yet more industrial capacity to that which already exists in Europe unless there is a clear comparative advantage in doing so – not something which can often be demonstrated in the case of the LDDI.

However, were the larger nations to consider it desirable to endure short-term economic disadvantage in the interests of longer-term gain, by aiding the LDDI nations, it is important that the penalties are recognized. For example, when LDDI nations join collaborative projects the work has to be spread more widely and the already higher costs of a collaborative development, though shared between a larger number of partners, are further increased.

The involvement of Spain as a minority (13%) partner in the development of the new European Fighter Aircraft (EFA) provides an example, even though Spain is not, in NATO terms, an LDDI nation. To the major EFA partners, the United Kingdom, Germany and Italy, there was no technological or financial advantage in having Spain as even a very junior member of the project in the development phase; quite the reverse. Politically, however, with Spain wavering in NATO on the one hand, but having joined the European Community and aspiring to membership of the Western European Union on the other, it was felt, particularly in London, that Spain should join the project if it wished. Having made maximum use of the bargaining strength given to it by the invitation at the same time to join the corresponding French *Rafale* project, Spain eventually became a partner in EFA.

The development arrangements agreed do not, however, make complete financial sense for the major EFA partners. In particular, Spain's weakness in aero-engine technology means that it will be unable to carry out enough work on this part of the project to fulfil even its modest 13% share. But *juste retour* still applies, and the consequence is that all the partners have had to agree to an economically inefficient compensation mechanism to make up the Spanish share. This matters scarcely at all to Spain. The overall project cost is increased but, with only a small liability, Spain is not greatly concerned; the wider benefits of participation in this advanced project far outweigh the cost penalties. For Spain, with barely concealed ambition to become the 'hi-tech sunshine state' of Europe, joining the EFA was worth almost any price.

The IEPG Action Plan
However, despite, or more probably because of the flaws in the Vredeling Report, ministers were able to instruct NADs to produce an Action Plan, with recommendations for the step-by-step creation of a European arms market. The recommendations did not have to be confined to those put forward by Vredeling. The resulting Plan, drawn up by German delegates to the IEPG, was accepted by NADs in July 1988 and endorsed by ministers the following November.

The Plan was in fact closely modelled on the Vredeling approach, particularly in its concerns with *juste retour* as 'a means to gain the support of member countries for a border-crossing competition' (sic),[4] but it was hoped that the goal of economy would prevail over demands for an exact return. Time will tell whether it does, but at least the Vredeling suggestion that the return should be achieved on a multi-project basis over a reasonable period of time was accepted.

As far as the LDDI nations are concerned, the Plan provides for the possibility of transition periods during which fledgling industries can be built up before borders are opened, and for positive discrimination in their favour. This is, no doubt, a realistic recognition that the smaller nations will not join the competitive game on any other basis. Whether it represents a cost-effective use of the equipment budgets of the larger countries is debatable.

Both *juste retour* and assistance to the LDDI featured largely in the ministerial communique which announced the adoption of the Action Plan. With these impediments still firmly in place, has any worthwhile progress been made? On balance, it appears that it has. Ministers have 'reaffirmed their determination' to create 'a European market for defence equipment'. They have also 'invited France to chair a new IEPG Panel, which will be tasked with the development of a European Technology Programme (ETP) and with considering how this might be funded in future.'[5] The ETP will be based on selected technological priority areas and will include the IEPG's current and future Co-operative Technology Projects (CTPs). The ETP, like the CTPs will be funded nationally, on a case-by-case basis. It is, however, this lack of common funding which has been the main reason for the poor showing of the CTPs to date. Although prolific in numbers (the UK alone is involved in 29), they have not yet proved very productive. There are serious bureaucratic obstacles to overcome before projects can be launched, and obtaining co-ordinated agreement from as many as seven nations to make a financial contribution is every bit as difficult as might be expected. The same problems beset the ETP, but its creation will give added momentum to the idea of co-operative military technology projects in Europe.

Making a plan does not of itself cause anything to happen as a result, even when the plan is endorsed at the highest level. The political pressure necessary to create the new economic order envisaged in the Action Plan will therefore need to be sustained for a long period. The small, newly-created IEPG secretariat has set about recording the workings of *juste retour* and promulgating the procurement and maintenance requirements of the nations in an agreed format, throughout the IEPG countries. This latter task, simple though it may sound, is proving remarkably difficult to accomplish. This does not bode well. More weighty activities, such as harmonizing bidding and contract award procedures, which are necessary preconditions to fair competition, have yet to be undertaken. This process could take years. Moreover, if cross-border competition begins to occur on a scale which seriously threatens national industries, especially in a context of decreased procurement spending, the political waverers might have second thoughts. There is already in some countries a less than whole-hearted enthusiasm for the UK's recent accession to the IEPG's Chair for a two-year period. They fear the consequences of what they regard as the UK's over-zealous adoption of a policy of competition in equipment procurement. But, for all the imperfections in the Action Plan and the difficulties there will be in implementing it, at least the principle of inter-European competition has been established. What is less clear is what European procurement policy should be with respect to the United States. The Plan is silent on that point.

Another omission is that the Plan does not call for machinery to be created to link it to the IEPG's primary function: harmonizing the nations' requirements with respect to specification and timescale. There must be a risk that attention will be diverted from this central task to the implementation of a Plan which will not, of itself, translate harmonized requirements into collective procurement action.

It could be argued, however, that because the work of the IEPG already substantially overlaps that of the CNAD, to which the Group contributes a 'European' view, the consequences of the IEPG taking its eye off the harmonization ball would not be unduly serious: CNAD is all that is needed anyway. Certainly there is duplication of effort between the two bodies, and time and human resources are wasted as a consequence. This fact, together with US fears about the outcome for its export sales of the establishment of an open European market, has already prompted complaints from NATO about the role of the IEPG and the way it works. Nonetheless, the vital importance of including

France in European arms planning, while it remains outside NATO's integrated military structure, means that for the foreseeable future there is no alternative to keeping the two groupings in being. It will therefore be imperative for the IEPG not to lose its way. This is particularly important because the IEPG enjoys one unique and vital strength. The adoption of the Action Plan means that the Group is well placed to deal with the EC's interest in arms transactions.

The IEPG and the European Commission
There seems little doubt that by the end of 1992 the European Council and the Commission will have largely completed the agenda they have set themselves for the establishment of an open internal market in Europe. For reasons discussed later, this is likely to be a less dramatic event than some ministers and Commissioners seek to suggest. Nonetheless, the creation of even a notional open market for public contracts will further highlight the provisions of Article 223 of the Rome Treaty,[6] 'which allows specifically military goods to bypass common market arrangements. Despite the special considerations which attend on nations' arms provision, it is hard to imagine such an obvious anomaly persisting indefinitely. Brussels makes no secret of its ambitions to leave no anomalies to cloud the vision of administrative harmony in European public procurement, and the Commission said in 1988 that it:

> now has to address as a matter of priority the question of defence procurement in the light of the provisions of both the EEC Treaty and the European co-operation provisions of the Single European Act with a view to the development of policy initiatives that will ensure the coherent realization of their objectives. Such initiatives will need to be considered by those responsible in the near future so that their adoption and implementation are in concordance with the realization of the internal market by 31 December 1992.[7]

Although these are very positive words, particularly in respect of timescale, they are probably no more than an initial statement of intent which can be modified in negotiation. On the other hand, there is no doubt that the Commission is genuinely concerned that its member nations are placing different interpretations on the nature of the military items covered by the very general and, in technological terms, archaic lists of exclusions from the public procurement provisions of the Rome Treaty. Problems arise, in particular, in the growth sector of items with dual military and civil applications. The problem of where to draw the line is very real, and it is by no means certain that nations have been bending the rules. However, the Commission has been sufficiently disquieted to launch a compliance directive, lest nations lose sight of the legal consequences of a failure to play fair.

In addition, with the US in mind, the Commission has been pressed by the French to impose a common external tariff on the import of small items of military hardware and accessories, in order to promote their procurement from within Europe. It it were to be successfully extended to sub-systems, such an arrangement could seriously damage US sales prospects in Europe. There could even be substantial cost increases on European projects already in hand because dual-use concerns have led to the suggestion from the Commission that duty should be imposed on the import of civil aircraft which have been converted to military use. US objections have been vehement.[8] These issues are delicate ones for relationships between European defence ministers and the Commission, which on the whole, defence ministers would prefer to keep at arm's length. Trading relations between Europe and the US are also threatened. Healthy competition between Europe and America on trade matters should spread as 1992 beckons. Commission moves to alter procedures for equipment procurement should not be allowed to thwart this process or to impede the rationalization of the defence industries in Europe.

The Action Plan is therefore timely. IEPG ministers can say, with some justice, that they have already set in motion the wheels to liberalize arms procurement in ways which, in practice, equate to the procedures states will follow, for the foreseeable future, in other areas of public procurement. The Commission may well take this point. It is more than likely that for a few years they will regard the implementation of the Action Plan as a sufficient step in the right direction, provided real progress is made. If they do, it will mean that defence ministers will be allowed breathing space to manage change gradually; promoting competition while their economies come to terms with the consequences of its application. Their enthusiasm for the task will no doubt be all the greater for the knowledge that the Commission will be watching their endeavours.

In the longer term the Commission's concern is likely to focus on the application in principle of those elements of the Action Plan concerned with *juste retour*. If nations can show convincing evidence that they are on the whole more concerned with obtaining the economic benefits of competition than planning for precise returns, and that their commitment to a truly open market in due course is genuine, the IEPG will probably be left to continue with the process of freeing the market. Officials believe that the Commission accepts that the IEPG is better suited to the task than it is itself.[9] However, there are some worrying signs of tension in certain IEPG fora, which reflect a difference of emphasis between the large and small nations on what lies at the heart of the Action Plan. France, the UK, and to a lesser extent, the FRG, see the drive towards competition as its main thrust and *raison d'être*. For them it contains no more than a polite nod in the direction of *juste retour*. Most of the smaller nations have clearly understood the emphasis to be reversed. For example, shortly after Spain agreed to take a 13% share in the EFA project, the Spanish Defence Minister, Narcís Serra, said that Spain would obtain guarantees from other countries about equivalent returns in orders for Spanish industry. There should be no net outflow of investment from Spain in the project.[10]

If such attitudes persist, and stage-managed collaboration suppresses competition too visibly for too long, the Commission may step in. The actions that it could take if it was dissatisfied with matters range from updating the list of items excluded from the Rome Treaty, with far narrower definitions being imposed, to demands for re-negotiation of the Treaty's provisions. The actions that it would take would be a function of its resources, its perception of the market distortion involved and its concerns for bureaucratic tidiness.

But any efforts that IEPG ministers may make to keep the Commission at bay will be wasted if national industries fail to respond to the new commercial opportunities that the opening of the European arms market will provide. And the economic and security benefits of improved co-ordination of arms planning will not be fully realized unless the defence industries use the stimulus created by the moves towards an open market to restructure so as to meet both the challenge of competition and the emergence of more demanding customers.

II. THE DEFENCE INDUSTRIES

Japan, France, the FRG, UK and the US top the non-communist league in their expenditures on defence, and the US dwarfs the other four. Its defence budget is some $300 bn, roughly two-and-a-half times greater than the combined budgets of the European NATO countries.[1] Within Europe, France, the FRG and the UK take the lion's share of collective defence commitment. The equipment expenditure of the three countries in 1989 is estimated to be about $30 bn or 70% of the European total.[2] Any analysis of present problems and assessment of possible future developments must therefore centre on the big four.

Character and size of the defence industries
It is frequently claimed, not least by their managements, that the defence industries are 'different'. The defence market does, of course, possess characteristics which are not found together in other consumer or industrial markets. For example, much is made of the fact that, if export sales are set aside, it has a single buyer – the government. The market is monopsonistic. Moreover, even export sales, which are themselves controlled by the exporting government through licences, end-user restrictions and bans on high technology transfer, can only be made to other governments. What is more, export potential is itself a function of what national governments choose to order from the industry to meet national requirements. It is this single buyer's direction of the technologies that his suppliers adopt which can be commercially harmful. Export demands, particularly those from Third World customers, may not match a more sophisticated home need and, since the development of whole systems to meet overseas market needs is unlikely to be profitable, companies' sales can be constrained. Moreover, some governments are only now beginning to frame their equipment requirements with an eye to the export sales potential of the resulting item. Another characteristic of such a market is that it allows governments to determine in the first instance how much they will spend on a given category of equipment, thus setting the boundaries for the whole market, and for its segments, and, it is sometimes suggested, the price that they are therefore prepared to pay.

Table 3: Defence Production: Average % exported 1984–89[3]

France	45
FRG	10
UK	33
US	10

These arguments have some force, but they can be exaggerated. For example, the baleful effects on exports of the existence of a monopsonistic home buyer is frequently overstated, as Table 3 shows. Furthermore, in Europe at least, the worst that is allowed to befall firms with a heavy involvement in defence and which are important to the armed services, when they suffer a commercial downturn, is a forced marriage. The partnership of a monopsonistic buyer and largely oligopolistic sellers has proved a cosy one, but the taxpayer has lacked the certainty that equipment procurement is on the basis of value for money.

Attention is often drawn to the lack of competition amongst defence suppliers. Within an individual nation, this is certainly true at the level of whole weapons-platforms (ships, aircraft etc.) and for such items as aero-engines and specialized materials and equipment, because creating and maintaining the ability to make these very high technology products is expensive. In Europe there is often only a single national firm with the required capability, and even that firm may need government support to survive. This is a situation which is unlikely to alter. Barriers to defence market entry and exit are extensive.

Another feature frequently noted is that the products traded in the defence market are highly specialized, often – but not necessarily – with very long development and production lead times. Weapons systems are complex and are designed and manufactured in small numbers at great cost to meet a precisely defined customer need. But, at the other extreme, boots and rifles, as well as electronic components, can be sold from a catalogue.

Finally, the defence market and its component industries require substantial capital investment, predominantly in jigs, tools and test equipment. The cost can be very high, but that does not render the industry unique. What is more, this investment is often funded, in whole or in part, by the sole government customer. This has led Gansler to note that US defence companies have been characterized by modest profit on sales but very high returns on capital employed, which has made defence an attractive business to be in.[4] The same pattern can be found in the UK and to a lesser degree in Europe. GEC, for example, has a historic return on capital employed of 43%, whilst the figure for the French company, Thomson CSF, is 22%.[5] Few capital-intensive companies in the civil sector can match these figures.

When all these factors are aggregated, it does not seem to be a straightforward proposition that there are enough special features of the defence market to make it so uniquely different from any other that it operates under and must be run by its own special rules. In the final analysis, it is the wide constituency of interests that its state customer has to serve, so limiting the scope for completely rational purchasing decisions, which forms the basis of the claim to special status made by major defence firms and their sub-contractors. Even the latter can in some cases be totally dependent on defence orders. But, of course, there is plenty of irrationality in other industrial buying decisions.

Whether or not it is right to regard them as a 'special case', defence companies, both public and privately owned, have enjoyed a considerable degree of government protection through an almost guaranteed flow of orders, limits on foreign ownership, and financial assistance in securing export orders. This is only to be expected, given the very high level of self-sufficiency nations have sustained. Self-sufficiency has been in part demanded by national policy, but today's national industries are also a legacy of the haphazard way in which they were developed after 1945. On both sides of the Atlantic, the lack of any co-ordinated plans for helping firms to adjust to peacetime levels of demand led to the maintenance of over-capacity and an inevitable slow and painful rationalization in the 1950s and 1960s, despite the stimulus of the Korean War and American involvement in Vietnam. The trend in all cases, which has continued to this day, was the formation of fewer, larger concerns, which could enjoy the benefits of economies of scale and learning. Rationalization in aerospace and ship-building has been particularly marked.

There the similarities between the US and European industries end. The key difference is the size of the market which the two sets of defence companies serve. The turnover of the US aerospace industry is more than double that of the European total. Its output is correspondingly large. There are some 24,000 combat aircraft in the world, of which the US has designed 55%, although a significant number of US-designed aircraft have been built under licence overseas.[6] The US alone has more than one-and-a-half times the combined combat aircraft inventories of the Common Market countries. In both military and civil sectors, large orders allow long production runs, which lead to lower unit costs, thus making larger orders affordable next time round.

The European picture is vastly different. The European armaments industries waste both technological and financial resources because no single nation's industry can aspire to, let alone achieve, the scale of efficiency and competitiveness which the size of the US market provides for its indigenous firms. Without overt or covert government support, firms in some sectors of the European market are not commercially viable. The problem is frequently most apparent in the larger companies, many of which are monopoly or near-monopoly suppliers to their national governments, where the nature of the business demands long production runs to minimize costs and optimize profits. In contrast, at sub-system and component level, small can be beautiful, with technical ingenuity and low overheads generating commercial success in both home and export markets. The software houses, the one new group of suppliers to the defence market who have broken the barriers to entry because of the demand for their skills and the lack of capital investment required, and because economies of scale scarcely apply, are another example of success.

The problem lies with the lead companies who, despite being winnowed down to one or two national flag-carriers, exhibit substantial over-capacity and duplication of effort. The scale of the problem of over-capacity is difficult to assess. For obvious commercial reasons companies do not advertise factory underloading. Nonetheless one measure is the amount of turnover on defence contracts available for sale: revenue on which, it can be assumed, it is no longer possible to earn an adequate profit. Thus, in continental Europe, despite the French company Thomson CSF's recent acquisition of most of Dutch Philips defence interests for some $160 m, some $700 m of the defence revenues of companies in Europe are believed to be for sale or otherwise 'in play'.[7] In the UK, following the GEC/Siemens successful combined bid for Plessey in which some $730 m worth of revenues changed hands, $1,200 m remains available, but with no queue of purchasers.[8] Against this background it is scarcely surprising that the Chairman of British Aerospace (BAe) has said that he cannot see 'more than three or four major European businesses remaining in the European defence equipment industry by the mid-nineties'.[9] Even in the US, recent industrial sales and reconstructions have involved assets of $5.8 bn.[10] And throughout the West the problems of the defence industries can only be compounded if progress in conventional arms reductions leaves good quality second-hand equipment for sale to developing countries at bargain prices.

Despite an increasingly competitive market at home and overseas, not all national flag-carriers recognize the changed environment they face. In some respects they cannot be blamed for their predicament. Successive governments have all too often manoeuvred them into the position where they have become, in today's parlance, part of the 'dependency culture'. But the cost of that dependence has now become too high for governments to be able to bear indefinitely. Defence dependency is most acute amongst the large platform contractors. Fifty-nine per cent of the turnover of the five largest makers of weapons-platforms in France, the FRG and the UK is generated by defence contracts, including exports, with relatively little variation between countries.[11] Though the figure is perhaps surprisingly low, their turnover from defence, totalling some $1,400 m, is vital to the survival of these firms, and with export orders becoming harder to win they will continue to look to their national governments to sustain them. However, for many other important suppliers, with the exception of Thomson CSF in France which is 90% defence-dependent, defence by no means dominates their business. Table 3 at p. 25 gives an indication of the range of defence dependency amongst European contractors. In the European electronics sector, for example, the major contractors in 1988 relied on defence for only 11% of their turnover. The corresponding figure for the US is 13%, although the companies are much larger in size. These very much lower figures reflect the diverse range of activities in which the enterprises are engaged. For them, defence is just one more market to be served.

In all too many cases the platform contractors do not have the luxury of broadly-based businesses which can compensate for reduced demand in one sector by expansion in another. It is the size of the equipment cake to be divided amongst these hungry giants which will determine whether, for example, Europe can continue to support four companies – Agusta, Westland, MBB and Aérospatiale – with the capability to design, develop and produce military helicopters. Indeed, can Europe any longer support five fixed-wing airframe producers, Aérospatiale, Dassault, MBB, BAe and SAAB?

Industry Sketches
UNITED STATES
The US domestic military equipment market is the largest in the West. American defence acquisition expenditure (defined as procurement and research, development, testing and evaluation (RDT&E), has averaged $100 bn annually throughout the 1980s. Procurement expenditure alone is some $78 bn in Financial Year 1989–90.[13] Figures compiled by NATO from governments' responses to the annual defence planning questionnaire, which uses rather restricted definitions of both procurement and total defence expenditure, show that the US spent an average of 25% of its defence budget on equipment between 1983 and 1987.[14] Although the percentage of total spending devoted to equipment by the UK and, in recent years, some LDDI nations is of the same order, the amount of money spent is much less.

Similar differences of scale are to be found between the European nations and the US in R&D, though problems of definition make close comparison hazardous. Half of all US R&D expenditure is funded by the Federal Government and two-thirds of government R&D support goes to military work. The European nations have for many years spent only about one-third of the amount spent by the US on military R&D. The resulting US technological lead over Europe in many areas of military R&D activity is well recognized, and has given its industry very substantial competitive advantages, though it is far from certain that even US levels of expenditure on research will enable it to maintain in future a technological lead across the board.

Whether US self-sufficiency in arms production is simply a function of the scale and efficiency of indigenous firms, or whether the US domestic market is effectively closed to foreign competition, is a matter of some debate. The US government points to regulations which should in theory make it amongst the most open in the world. French and UK firms point to the fact that, although they have won orders in some sectors on recent years through offering unarguably superior technology, sustained attempts to bring the arms-trade balance between Europe and the US closer to parity have met with only partial success.

There has been considerable recent speculation that the US market will become more open with the creation of a single European market, because US firms fear exclusion from Europe, despite official assurances that there will be no 'fortress Europe'. The consensus judgement is that a fight for survival will lead to greater reciprocity, not least because of the importance of the European Community to US industry. The total US economic stake in the EC is enormous. The Community accounts for 24% of US exports, 40% of its foreign investment and between 60 and 70% of its defence exports.[15] The US, as the largest debtor nation in the world, with a budget deficit in Fiscal Year 1989 of $152 bn, cannot afford to pass up the export growth opportunities that an integrated European market should provide.

However, although the proportion of US arms exports going to Europe is large, US arms producers have traditionally been far less reliant on exports than their European counterparts, despite the wide trade imbalance between the two markets and the fact that the US is the largest arms exporter in the West, with a world market share of around 28%.[16] Military exports currently account for only 10% of US defence firms' business, though their high value makes the US dependent on arms for 5% of its total exports. The major US electronic companies, embracing defence systems as well as computers and telecommunications export, on average, no more than 15% of their production to Europe, and 24% in total. In contrast, the major UK electronics firms are thought to export 39% of their defence output, while the engineering companies export 63%. Together, these two sectors represent 87% of UK procurement expenditure.[17] Increasingly, however, constraints on US defence spending may lead its industries to seek to push the proportion of their turnover derived from defence exports closer to European levels. There are early indications that in pursuit of this aim, US firms are being encouraged to fight for business on competitive commercial terms, rather than having to include the cost of government assistance in their prices.

If its intention is to sell harder abroad, the US defence industry has more than a head start over European firms. The US companies serve a market many times larger than that of the European total, using a common language and common currency. Its main customer, the US government, is able to follow what is, by European standards, a coherent procurement policy through which competing military requirements are phased, co-ordinated and matched more closely to budget provision. This is not to suggest that the system is by any means perfect. In particular, the need for Congress to renew each year its funding approval for major equipment purchases introduces planning and production inefficiencies. It also complicates collaborative arrangements. Nor is there any substantive evidence that the system leads to more effective public oversight and control of defence equipment programmes. The US has its share of projects which go technically or financially out of control. Nevertheless, the US defence industry as a whole enjoys an inherent competitive advantage.

As in Europe, the US defence industry is characterized by system companies with no overwhelming degree of dependence on defence business, largely free to come and go as they please in accordance with their perception of profit opportunities. Even for some of the largest platform contractors such as Boeing and McDonnell Douglas, defence business is not critical to survival. But there are others with a total or substantial degree of dependence on defence contracts, which must make them uneasy. If Europe is asking itself whether it has room for five large aerospace companies, some with good export records, America must be wondering how long it can support six, some with poor export records, particularly when the resulting over-capacity gives rise to inefficiencies which have been estimated to cost $3.5 bn a year (at 1980 prices).[18] In classical economic terms, of course, the fact that a number of suppliers exist, from amongst whom a competitive selection can be made, should keep prices down. The question is whether if the number of potential platform suppliers is allowed to fall, thereby raising levels of industrial concentration, this would introduce inefficiencies greater than the cost of maintaining the existing over-capacity.

The US DIB has already experienced marked shrinkage. In 1982 the majority of US requirements were met by some 118,000 firms. By 1987 only 38,000 firms supplied the same range of goods, even though over this period the procurement budget had grown by 58% at constant prices.[19] Many factors have contributed to this change. In general it would seem that declining profit rates, increasing risk and programme uncertainties, combined with the prospect of declining defence budgets, have caused US defence firms to pursue profits elsewhere or step up their efforts to export. For the customer this means less choice and less scope for competition.

A particularly striking feature of the US defence industry scene is that its firms and their customers have in the past gained from the production efficiencies which flow from orders which are typically five or six times larger than the orders from individual European nations to their national firms. Keith Hartley has noted that these production learning curves are an important determinant of efficiency in aircraft production.[20] Development costs can be spread over a larger number of units, production costs fall as the workforce learns how to do its work quicker or more efficiently, and it becomes more cost-effective to use the latest production technology. These factors are common across a wide spectrum of defence equipment. They have given the US a significant advantage in high technology weapons with long production runs.

Some of these advantages may be lost in future as the spiral turns downwards with ever-increasing costs leading to the purchase of fewer units which in turn leads to uneconomic production rates, so contributing to a further rise in unit costs. Even before the Berlin Wall was breached, US defence planners were concerned about whether there are both affordable and economic ways of producing militarily efficient quantities of B-2 bombers. It may well be that the resulting adjustments to equipment programmes will prompt further structural change in the US defence industry.

FRANCE

'The French objective is a complete control of an industry capable of meeting the national defence requirements'.[21] Although this objective is not met fully in practice, France comes the closest of the European nations to achieving self-sufficiency in arms production. The reasons for adopting this increasingly expensive policy are woven deeply into the social and political fabric of the nation. Long-standing French concerns to maintain independence and control of its own security requires autonomous military forces who are beholden to no one in respect of equipment or anything else. The central French defence concern is to maintain the means nationally to deter or deal with an attack on the country itself. Secondly, there is a policy of providing for the defence of overseas territories in which French influence remains strong. This is also a role which, perhaps more obviously, must be capable of being carried out independently.

The consequence has been, following a post-1945 reconstruction of the French defence industries, and various periods of consolidation and government-managed restructuring, a need in the 1980s to take the key firms into what is effectively public ownership as the only way to maintain a high degree of national self-reliance.

Inward direction of equipment expenditure, coupled with increases in French defence expenditure over the last 15 years, has helped to maintain a broad spectrum of industrial capability, which reflects the breadth of independent military operations which France believes it should be in a position to mount. Approximately one-third of French procurement expenditure is directed to its independent nuclear deterrent. France's combined nuclear forces require not only weapons but also sophisticated command and control systems and the delivery platforms – nuclear submarines and bombers. French industry can build all these, just as, on the conventional side, they can and do offer a full and diverse range of aircraft, armoured vehicles and warships. But the price of keeping such a broad industrial capability in a country with an annual equipment budget roughly comparable to that of the UK, has been pronounced industrial concentration. Indeed, the creation of a concentrated industry has been an objective of the *Délégation Générale pour l'Armement* (DGA), the organization within the Ministry of Defence for researching, developing and producing defence equipment and systems, since it was set up in 1961. Relations between government and the defence industry in France are the closest of any of the four major arms producers within the Alliance – perhaps too close. Be that as it may, the DGA, through its research and procurement policies, contractor selection and industrial funding exerts formidable control over the French defence industry. This close direction of a concentrated industry in turn allows the DGA considerable discretion in determining the equipment needs of the French services. For example, it is an arms manufacturer in its own right and virtually a monopoly supplier in land and sea systems. It also has an aircraft and helicopter repair capability. Some indication of the scale and spread of its activities is given by the size of its workforce – some 73,000 in 1986. Its manufacturing tasks alone put it on a footing with industrial groups such as Elf-Aquitaine and Michelin.

However, in aerospace and electronics, separate industrial companies dominate, though the large shareholding that the state has in nearly all of them make them, either in law or in practice, nationalized industries. And even here DGA subventions have in the past meant that the contractor's financial risk has been very small. Moreover, state direction has created further *de facto* monopoly suppliers in this area – Aérospatiale for helicopters and ballistic missiles, Dassault for combat aircraft and Thomson CSF for major sensing systems. Across the whole of the defence industries the scale of concentration is such that, excluding DGA, the ten largest organizations account for over 60% of armament revenue.[22] This inevitably makes the organizations involved heavily dependent on defence contracts. Sixty-four per cent of aerospace sales and 55% of electronics revenue come from armaments.

Surprisingly, taking the French defence industry as a whole, concentration does not appear to have led to very great productivity gains, at least in comparison to the UK. The two countries have industries of very different character, and France spends some 15–20% more on equipment than the UK, yet it employs 281,000 people in its defence industries (1.2% of the working population) and the UK 260,000 (1.6% of the working population)[23].

The two countries are also comparable in the effort that they devote to arms exports as a means of increasing production runs, so lowering the unit costs of their own purchases and strengthening the commercial position of their industries. Where they differ is that the UK rarely uses actual or potential arms exports as an active instrument of foreign policy. France is more inclined to do so.

It was a combination of emphasis on arms exports as a vehicle for exporting French influence and the pressing need to find ways of paying for its policy of near self-sufficiency which led France to market its wares aggressively and to become, until recently, the leading arms exporter in Europe. (The UK will be in the lead provided the second of its two *Al Yamamah* oil-barter deals with Saudi Arabia, estimated to be worth $25 bn over the period 1986–97, comes to fruition). France achieved this position partly because its equipment specifications are geared to its perceived need to have an intervention capability in Third World countries, notably Africa. This in turn makes the items readily exportable.

Traditionally, the main customers for French exports have been Egypt, Jordan, Iraq and Saudi Arabia. They are so no longer. Export success has left French industry exposed to the consequences of shifts in world markets. Just as the US saw its share of the world market drop by some 40% between 1976 and 1986, as competition grew, so France is having to adjust not only to aggressive marketing by the UK at the more sophisticated end of the market, but also to the consequences of fresh waves of competition from countries with newly created arms industries – Brazil, India, Israel and Korea – offering relatively low technology and therefore cheap products. Arms industries now exist in 36 Third World countries. In addition, the drop in oil prices has made Middle Eastern petro-dollars harder to come by. The consequences are threefold: France is having to search out new markets, notably in South-east Asia; co-operation with other European countries, especially in research, is very much on the agenda; and cuts are having to be made in the expensive multi-year national equipment pro-gramme. The immediate shopping list for the latter included a nuclear-powered aircraft carrier, new and refurbished SSBNs, several dozen short-to-medium range land-based nuclear missile launchers, 1,400 *Leclerc* tanks (a programme already afflicted by delays and cost overruns and with the size of buy now being reduced) the Franco-German combat helicopter and 330 *Rafale* fighter aircraft. The French Prime Minister has called the estimated $19 bn cost of these aircraft 'catastrophic'.[24] In the longer term, France aspires to a carrier battle group. For all these programmes to have been completed according to the original plan, weapons expenditure would have had to grow at around 6% above the level of inflation for a sustained period. Sufficient funds were unlikely to be forthcoming. Savings of over $6 bn in planned French defence expenditure over the next four years were announced in mid-1989.[25]

While the political and diplomatic investment in these very high profile projects is such that none of them is yet a candidate for immedi-ate outright cancellation, it is already necessary for France to stretch procurement timescales and cancel some smaller programmes. Industrially, this will further increase existing over-capacity in the aerospace sector and magnify the already severe problems faced by the government's armaments factories, which are concentrated in the less auspicious heavy engineering sectors and often located in economi-cally depressed areas. As a recent French government report has con-cluded, 'one or two industrial companies will stay in certain sectors, but others will either have to abandon entire branches, or have to give up prime contracting by finding cooperation abroad.'[26]

GERMANY
Although the FRG remains the junior partner amongst the major European arms producers, its equipment expenditure, estimated to amount in 1989 to some $8.1 bn,[27] is still substantial. The country mir-rors its major European partners in allocating some 85% of this expenditure to its indigenous industry. This has led to the creation of industrial capacity of the same order as France and the UK. Some

250,000 people, 1% of the working population, are employed in the FRG's defence companies. Their output accounts for 1% of Gross Domestic Product and the defence production share of manufacturing output ranges between 2 and 3%. In the FRG, as in France, the US and the UK, neither manufacturing industry nor the economy as a whole are vitally dependent on the armaments industry.

Germany's level of industrial concentration is high. Following separate disposal of its naval technology interests, Messerschmidt-Bolkow-Blohm (MBB), the country's flag-carrying airframe and defence equipment manufacturer, which is owned by the provincial governments and is itself a relatively recent product of government-contrived aircraft company mergers, is being absorbed by Daimler Benz, Germany's largest industrial company, which will then account for some 40% of the FRG's defence-procurement expenditure. Fifty-seven per cent of MBB's revenue comes from defence. But even though its defence sales rank third in Europe after BAe and Aérospatiale, at $1.8 bn annually,[28] it will be a minnow in the Daimler Benz pond. Daimler Benz has projected annual sales, following the merger, of $46 bn and currently relies on defence for only 4% of its revenue, even though its recently-acquired Dornier, AEG and MTU subsidiaries have defence interests. German defence companies are also involved in cross-border restructuring. The German company Siemens joined with the UK's GEC to mount a successful hostile bid for the UK telecommunications and defence company, Plessey. Matra, the French defence and electronics group, has taken a 20% stake in BGT, the FRG's leading manufacturer of air-to-air missiles. These are typical examples of the volatility of the relationships between major industrial contractors and the rapid developments in the formation of transnational industrial groups.

Despite its high level of self-sufficiency in arms production, the FRG, together with its major European allies, is dependent in large measure on externally-sourced components to incorporate in the systems its industry produces. Even US manufacturers are beginning to experience this dependency. Self-sufficiency in arms production is increasingly becoming more apparent than real. However, this has not deterred the West German government from pursuing a policy directed at building up national capabilities through enthusiastic participation in European collaborative projects. Approximately one-third of the equipment projects West Germany has in train are bi-national or multinational. Sixty per cent of the country's development expenditure is directed at collaborative programmes. Collaboration is explained in the 1985 German Defence White Paper (its most recent) as a means of strengthening Alliance cohesion, while an indigenous manufacturing capacity is said to minimize dependence on others and generate civil spin-off.[29] But collaboration is also a means of reinforcing the FRG's ties with key allies and influencing their actions, with the added benefit that *juste retour* arrangements have led to a marked increase in the share of weapons for the *Bundeswehr* manufactured domestically rather than purchased abroad. Perhaps it is because of this that the same White Paper specifically mentions that the FRG does not, however, seek self-sufficiency in military research and technology, and its industry has in the past relied heavily on licensing US technology. Under steady government direction, Germany's defence firms have flourished and the country is now beginning to feel that its capabilities are the equal of the larger European nations. Collaboration between equals is never easy.

As well as giving influence, collaboration brings industrial benefits, particularly for countries with industries at a relatively infant stage. The German aerospace industry is a case in point. Participation in the *Tornado* combat aircraft programme meant the transfer to Germany of a great deal of technical information and know-how, as well as the establishment of new production facilities. The immediate consequence is that the German aerospace industry is up to date and efficient. The longer-term consequence is that, as with any of the major producers, it will only stay that way if follow-on projects can be found and funded.

On the question of funding, the FRG will not be immune from the pressure on the proportion of defence expenditure devoted to supply and resupply that is and will be increasingly common amongst Alliance partners. The FRG spends approximately one-third of its defence funds on 'investment' i.e. R&D, procurement and infrastructure. Although, again, problems of definition make comparisons tricky, this is less than the UK or France. However, the figure is set to increase in the next few years to around 36% to finance Germany's substantial commitment to new equipment buys. But, because, *inter alia*, of the costs associated with the unification of Germany and the consequences thereof, this goal may not be achieved. 'Big-ticket' equipment programmes, including collaborative projects, if they are not abandoned, may therefore need to be stretched into the first decade of the next century, with damaging financial consequences for German defence companies and their collaborative partners. The affordability of the EFA programme, the Franco-German PAH-2 attack helicopter project, as well as the planned replacement for the *Leopard* 2 main battle tank are already increasingly being questioned. Moreover, although Germany is the third largest net exporter of arms in Europe, with particular strengths in land and sea systems, its political legacy has meant that its direct export business is dwarfed by those of the UK and France. Exports do not therefore deflect the effects of pressures on the German equipment budget.

It has already been noted that the UK is pursuing a policy of competition between defence contractors to secure value for money and alleviate budgetary pressures and France is now following suit with some vigour. The FRG too is becoming attracted to fixed price contracts obtained through competitive tendering, though it is still hesitant about taking this route in respect of major weapons-platforms. However, it now faces something of a dilemma. With Daimler Benz absorbing 40% of its equipment expenditure, a far higher proportion than BAe in the UK, the scope for national competition is limited. Paradoxically, institutional arrangements exist to preserve competition in the German economy. All mergers and acquisitions which create a market share for a single firm in excess of 20% must, by law, be referred to the Federal Cartel Office (whose advice was overridden in the case of Daimler Benz's absorption of MBB). So now, if it is to enjoy the full benefits of competitive procurement and thus reduce its budget exposure, Bonn may have to look to buying more from overseas.

Such a shift of emphasis, if it occurs, is unlikely to be marked. As international competition intensifies, the FRG's indigenous industry can be expected to continue to be favoured, despite the free market ideology professed in varying degrees by successive federal governments. International competitiveness will still be sought through the state-supported transfer of resources into knowledge or technology-intensive industrial sectors. For example, substantial support is being given to defence-related electronics, which has left AEG well placed in the military radar market. The deeply-rooted German ambivalence about arms exports may, nonetheless, be expected to continue to cause periodic political difficulties.

UNITED KINGDOM

The UK defence industry total annual sales are reasonably constant at around $21 bn. Within this total, exports account for a little over one-quarter. Fifty-one per cent of UK sales abroad are to the Middle East and North Africa. Defence exports account for about 3% of total UK sales overseas. According to government figures, 60,000 people are directly employed in defence companies on export contracts. Sub-contractors and other suppliers to the main contractors employ a further 50,000 on export work.[30]

A handful of large contractors, either privately owned or returned to private ownership in recent years, dominate the scene. Although 8,000 companies are Ministry of Defence (MOD) 'approved', the industry exhibits the classic pattern in which 20% of suppliers win 80% of the available market. Some idea of the level of concentration can be gauged from the fact that in 1986–7 the MOD paid only six contractors more than $425 m, whereas 44 companies earned between $8.5 m and $17 m.[31] Even though a great deal of this work will have been sub-contracted to smaller firms, the value of many MOD contracts awarded to the other 7,900 or so approved firms is relatively small. Of course, this could still leave them dependent on defence work, but a broadening of the UK DIB in recent years to bring in more small firms – the so-called Small Firms Initiative, intended to secure improved value for money by using suppliers with low overheads – will have the effect of slightly reducing concentration.

Setting aside the essential but non defence-specific suppliers of food, fuel, clothing and the like, the UK defence industry, like that of other leading arms producers, divides into two key sectors: engineering, which in 1988–9 was planned to absorb some $7 bn (nearly half the UK's procurement expenditure), and electronics, on which some $5 bn was planned to be spent in 1988–9 (one-third of procurement expenditure). Both figures are reductions in real terms over the previous year, and in the case of engineering the fall is greater than the 4% overall drop in UK defence expenditure in real terms. The disproportionate drop in equipment expenditure is primarily a result of growing manpower costs to be accommodated within a defence budget which is declining as a proportion of an expanding GDP. If this trend continues, and *a fortiori* if, as seems likely, it steepens as a consequence of conventional force reductions in Europe, it will obviously have a marked effect on the fortunes of defence contractors and the long-term structure of the DIB. The effect would be extensive in the case of the major indigenous electronic and missile suppliers, who prospered throughout the 1980s when their products took a steadily larger proportion of equipment expenditure at the expense of large companies making weapons-platforms. Already, in some procurement sectors, platform contractors have found revenues down in real terms by as much as 30% on a few years ago. A similar pattern of system expansion at the cost of platform decline can be seen in the FRG and France.

Although it does not sacrifice conventional equipment to meet nuclear requirements to the same extent as France, the UK's conventional expenditure will be held down until the mid-1990s by the need to fund its new $15.3 bn strategic submarine deterrent system, *Trident*. Expenditure on *Trident* is set to run at between $1.7 bn and $2.0 bn for each of the three years until 1992. This is about 6% of the UK's overall defence budget and about 12% of the total planned equipment spend. Although US industry will supply the *Trident* missiles and their launch and control systems, 65–70% of this expenditure will be with UK industry.

The UK government's answer to criticism of the negative trends and patterns in equipment spending is that there is no need for concern about the future of the UK DIB. It argues that a more commercial approach to procurement by sharpening industrial competitiveness at home and abroad leaves the DIB better able to withstand adverse trends. Nonetheless, there has been a marked disinclination to settle the matter one way or the other by exposing UK defence firms to international procurement competition for any sustained period. At best there has been the occasional sacrifice *pour encourager les autres.* From the contractors' viewpoint, even though they are largely insulated from international competition in the home market, prospects are dull, margins are under pressure and export sales, though still attractive, are difficult to win. It is a familiar picture in all advanced arms-producing countries.

However, there are wide variations in company exposure to defence spending in both the engineering and electronic sectors, even though, overall, in both groups, defence sales account for 30% of the revenue of major companies. In general, the UK's large defence companies are more dependent on defence, counting both home and export sales, than their counterparts in the US and the FRG, but less so than the 'private' French aerospace companies. Within the aerospace sector, where BAe, with a turnover of $9.0 bn (civil and military) dominates and Westland and Shorts are major players, defence absorbs about half the output. In shipbuilding, where defence orders are split between the submarine constructor Vickers, Cammell Laird and Yarrow, the figure is one-third. Estimates in the electronics sector, in which GEC (with sales of $9.3 bn), Plessey, Racal and STC lead, are more variable. Figures range from 15–30%, with official estimates tending towards the higher end of the range.[32]

With the notable exceptions of BAe, Ferranti and Westland Helicopters, defence work is subordinate to civil business amongst major UK defence contractors. A recent survey of 40 of the MOD's contractors, representative of all sizes of company and types of manufacture and research, with an aggregated turnover of $42 bn, revealed that they relied on defence for 32% of their sales.[33] Declining defence expenditure in real terms, and a readily detectable trend for defence suppliers to diversify away from defence where they can, suggest that this figure will fall.

Where defence business remains important, the ability of contractors, particularly those newly privatized, to adjust to a drop in government spending varies both between the two key sectors of engineering and electronics and between the companies within those sectors. For example, the UK's major defence supplier and Europe's largest aerospace company, BAe, ranks only sixth in the world in terms of turnover, with five US aerospace firms ahead of it. Like its European counterparts it therefore remains relatively vulnerable to US technological challenge, but unlike them a foreign shareholding as high as 29% is possible. Another company in the engineering sector, the aero-engine company, Rolls-Royce, with defence business about one-third that of BAe, finds it difficult to break the US grip on orders from continental Europe and its successful civil business in the US remains vulnerable to any protectionism prompted by moves towards a European defence market.

It is in electronics, more than any other industrial sector, that the contemporary trend towards the establishment in major companies of a broad technological base, serving both civil and military markets, can most readily be seen. Until early 1990 six companies dominated the UK field, with all six having some degree of military radar design and production capability. However none of them had the resources or the capability to develop unaided the next generation of radars – adaptive phased array systems. This is because the indigenous UK electronics industry, in both civil and military spheres, has from a commercial viewpoint, been unhealthily fragmented. Nonetheless, in the defence field it is the strongest and most comprehensive in Europe, a situation which may be further improved by GEC's acquisition of Ferranti's defence division in January 1990.

Table 4: Ownership of selected European defence contractors[34]

Firm	Average Sales ($m)	% Defence	Ownership
France			
Aérospatiale	3,350	77	Government
Dassault	2,100	66	49% family 46% government
Matra	2,400	38	Recently privatized public company; (Daimler Benz and GEC 10% each)
Thomson CSF	4,800	90	57% government
FRG			
Daimler Benz	33,600		Public company (Kuwait 14%)
MBB	2,800	57	Principally provincial governments. Purchased by Daimler Benz in 1989
Rheinmetall	1,370	37	Public company
SEL	2,600	11	Bought by CGE of France in 1987
Siemens	23,600	2	Public company
UK			
BAe	9,000	56	Recently privatized public company (overseas holdings limited to 29%)
Ferranti International Signal	1,500	80	Public company
GEC	9,320	38	Public company
Racal	2,200	18	Public company

In the past ten years, foreign companies have established a very strong position in the UK, and indigenous companies have failed to hold their market share, as well as growing more slowly than their foreign competitors. This slower rate of growth is partly a function of a failure to reinvest, but the National Economic Development Office (NEDO) has argued that another reason for it is the, by international standards, high concentration by UK electronics companies in defence electronics and telecommunications.[35] These have been, on average, among the slowest growing sectors in the electronics industry worldwide. Amongst major UK electronics firms in 1976, there was an aggregated 48% dependence on defence and telecommunications; by 1986 this had risen to 57%. (The figure for US and European companies was 24%, though even here there is growing evidence of defence dependence.) For some UK companies this shift was a conscious strategy to ensure survival by building a bigger stake in the secure if unexciting environment of a protected defence market. Others drifted into an undesirable degree of defence dependence through failure to compete either at home or abroad. However, the defence sector will at best be static in volume terms for some years. In addition, tougher procurement policies may well erode margins further. At the same time, UK firms have lost out to foreign competition in the most global sectors of the electronics market.

There is only one viable solution to these problems: restructuring and consolidation to pool resources in large pan-national combined defence and civil electronic groupings in which the two parts are interdependent. The only matter for discussion is the means by which it should be brought about. This raises more general questions about the costs and benefits of maintaining national DIBs and what their future should be.

The case for a base

It has been suggested that in the case of the UK, the 'MOD can either procure weapons or maintain the DIB – not both'.[36] The position is not yet so grave that such stark choices have to be made. But the factors that allow the choice to be posed are real and they are present in the other major European arms-producing nations. Moreover, as less economically developed countries build up their defence industries, they are establishing for themselves the basis of the same dilemma in future years.

The pressures are already provoking some change in national arms procurement practice, away from high levels of support for home industries to obtaining better value for money through international competition. France and the UK, for example, have adopted a policy of reciprocal purchasing, and both countries have bought US AWACS aircraft. How far this pressure can and should go will depend upon the view that governments take of the importance of national DIBs. It has already been noted that autarchy in defence production, though apparently considerable at the system level, is less substantial at the subsystem level, and in some cases surprisingly low when it comes to components. There is also considerable reliance on US technology. Thus, although France has the capacity to develop and produce *Rafale* and the UK has the capacity, though not the cash, to make EFA by itself, such systems would in any event incorporate many foreign parts. The air defence variant of the *Tornado* relied on an American radar, and its non-European content overall is variously estimated at between 20 and 35%.

The case for maintaining a national DIB rests on two sets of factors – strategic and economic. In respect of the former, a national DIB is said to give independence and security. Such logic as the argument possesses points to the need for complete self-sufficiency. But it is not a logic which all nations pursue – they cannot afford to. It is, of course, easier to tailor equipment precisely to service needs through using national firms and this may increase operational efficiency, at least in theory, though standardization and interoperability may be at risk. However, bespoke tailoring is a luxury few can afford. Moreover, in a world of growing technical and industrial interdependence, is it sensible to worry overmuch about foreign sources of supply except in economic terms? Of course, many countries deem certain items militarily vital: communications and cypher equipment, for example, or nuclear technology. In these cases, the capability to make them has to be available. But the truly vital needs of any nation are limited and the industrial capacity they require, together with its costs, can only be justified if it is possible to predict with accuracy what future vital requirements might be: a notoriously difficult task. Common sense suggests that the argument that 'you never know what we might need' has some validity. The problem lies in putting a value on it, and thus deciding whether it is better to pay the cost of the insurance or to accept the risk. Moreover in practice it is hard to pin down the size of the insurance premium because the cost of alternative policies cannot be accurately assessed. Another important strategic consideration is that current NATO planning is primarily based on short-war scenarios with nations fighting with what they have, for budgetary reasons as much as anything else. The contribution that indigenous industrial capacity can make to independence and security in war is therefore limited. Only in a protracted conventional war will there be time for industry to manufacture for resupply to maintain national fighting capabilities or to 'surge' to increase rates of supply if equipment needs have been underestimated.

Of course there will always be unexpected military contingencies like the Falklands War. Tributes have been paid to the inspired improvization of the UK's defence contractors and their ability to jury-rig equipment to meet unforeseen operational needs which arose in that conflict. There is no doubt that much good work was done which would perhaps not have been possible without industrial experience and competence, though it is less certain that it made the difference between victory and defeat. But it is uncertainty that makes it tempting on strategic grounds to retain the capacity 'just in case'.

The economic arguments for preserving a DIB are at least clearer and more quantifiable, even if they have not been fully evaluated. First there is the matter of employment, which has two aspects: the sheer number of jobs that defence spending generates and their locations and the economic consequences of using manpower in this way. The 1–2% of the workforce occupied in the defence industries in the major European countries are significant, but not as significant as many assert. For example, when the UK cancelled the $1,200 m *Nimrod* AEW programme only 2,000 jobs were lost at the main contractor and nearly half the people were re-employed by the same firm within a month.[37] Moreover, the capital-intensive nature of the defence industries means that its jobs are expensive to create. This is one economic inefficiency which causes concern. The other is the quality of the manpower the defence industries absorb, which is therefore unavailable for more 'productive' work in the civil field. Between 30 and 50% of the workforce in an aerospace or electronics company will be qualified engineers or scientists. Only in very high technology civil fields do companies have anything like the same profile. Defence companies therefore take a disproportionate share of a nation's technical manpower. The extent to which this poses a real economic penalty, which could be avoided, is the subject of a complex (and unresolved) argument, which involves questions ranging from whether people choose to work in defence companies because their projects are at the forefront of technology and they would not be so productive in civil work, to whether it is feasible in any case to run defence work down and transfer to something else. If so, to what? And how long would this process take and how much would it cost? Impending conventional force cuts may oblige people to find answers to these questions. It is hard to believe that they are unanswerable.

Compounding this question of optimum use of manpower is the fact that in the UK there will be 30% fewer school leavers by 1995, and 35% less in the FRG and Italy by 2010. National defence industries may therefore find it difficult to sustain themselves at their present size, whatever happens.

The foreign exchange savings and earnings which a national DIB produces are further economic factors of some significance. Their importance obviously depends on the trade balance in each country and, if its economy runs to a deficit in manufactured goods, whether it is a net importer or net exporter of defence materiel. The UK, for example, has a considerable and growing overall trade deficit. It imports only 10% of its equipment requirements, yet when imported raw materials, participation in collaborative projects and imported sub-systems are taken into account, the average imported element in UK equipment is found to be around 25%. This is one of the reasons why the UK promotes defence exports so vigorously, why it is placing increasing emphasis on making the equipment its services buy more exportable, and why its success in the high value aerospace sector is so important. Although it is impossible to identify the true balance, MOD's figures indicate that at present the value of defence exports exceeds the value of imports by nearly 3:1, although these data are thought to understate imports by a wide margin.[38] Nonetheless, the actual balance is probably favourable.

But all exporting countries face difficult times ahead and the need to find new ways of doing business as overseas markets shrink and more large orders, like the UK's two *Al Yamamah* deals, seem likely to be done on the basis of counter-trading, (in this case oil barter – which created still-unresolved difficulties when oil prices fell). Importing countries now normally require the exporter to buy from them goods, usually high technology military items, to compensate for the employment foregone and the foreign currency expended. Offset arrangements of this kind can and do add to the cost of the import, even though the seller selects his suppliers competitively. However they act to neutralize negative effects on the balance of payments. Without offset schemes or counter-trade arrangements, balance of payments considerations would seriously hamper international arms trade and limit the potential for international competition. To some extent they already do. The question to be answered is whether minimizing trade deficits is worth more to an economy than paying a price premium to support and buy from national companies.

One reason why nations pursue the national option lies in demanding military specifications requiring today's or, as specifiers frequently find, tomorrow's technology, which means that many defence companies are centres of technological excellence in R&D. And taking and holding the technological high ground is vital to the future of all industrialized nations. Knowledge is not only power: it is also prosperity.

Once knowledge has been gained, nations and firms are disinclined to share it. Hence the duplication of much military R&D activity. It is doubly unfortunate therefore that this activity is often massively expensive. Moreover, the less costly 'research' element is all too often rarefied, with little relevance to the economically far more important civil sector. Nonetheless, technological developments originating from defence requirements do provide a stimulus for industry at large, in the form of new materials and processes, devices and manufacturing techniques.

Apologists for the defence industries frequently try to talk up this civil spin-off from defence R&D. With the notable exception of aerospace, they have something of a hard time of it. Believing that there might be technologies developed in national R&D centres with unexploited civil potential, the UK government oversaw in 1985 the creation of Defence Technology Enterprises, a private company charged with the profitable transfer of military work to civil markets. Early results show that they have much work yet to do. Research amongst 40 UK defence companies, which absorb 65% of MOD's annual funding of industrial R&D, revealed that whilst they had over $27 bn of civil sales, only 20% of this figure was generated from defence technology.[39] Over half of these defence-derived civil sales

44

were to the aerospace market, because this is one of the few areas in which there is considerable overlap between the technical and manufacturing requirements of the two sectors.

Although there may be more intra-national spin-offs than these figures reveal, it seems that there is a considerable way to go before it can be concluded that continuing to direct public investment towards defence companies, sustaining them as an important repository of a nation's technological seed-corn, is the right way of ensuring that the resulting expertise diffuses through the whole of the manufacturing sector of the economy. Though much can be achieved through common technological bases, it is, after all, only military processes and not military products that can (or should) be transferred.

But above all else, it is the sheer cost of maintaining a broad spectrum of industrial capability which is now creating a procurement dilemma. Even the US, despite the size of its defence budget and its concerns over depending on foreign sources, has come to recognize that 'today's global economy no longer affords us the luxury of total self-sufficiency for all our industrial and material requirements' although co-operative projects will only be entered into 'in a manner that provides maximum benefit to the United States'.[40] It is this self-interested caveat which is symptomatic of attitudes, almost universally.

The hope for the future must be that existing defence industrial resources can be better organized in a properly functioning market to improve productivity, that the policies applied in it are shared and that they will be fairly and consistently applied.

III. PROCUREMENT PRACTICE

Equipment requirements are, in theory, determined solely by the assessment of new or altered threats. In practice the equipment response is bounded by the indigenous industrial capacity available to a nation, and what it can secure on world markets. However, that does not obviate the need for clear and consistent national procurement policies. With the exception of France, where, historically, the policy of self-sufficiency has been clear, firmly stated and articulated policies are rare. For example, in the US it was recently concluded that:

> Present US policies towards the defence industrial base . . . are largely ineffective. The effective policies that do exist are haphazardly applied and underfunded.[1]

In the UK the policy has to be deduced from procurement practice, which is not consistent but appears to lean towards buying from home suppliers, even at some additional cost, provided that cost is not too high and the technology benefit arguments are adequately persuasive. Jobs are now a diminished factor in the decision equation except in marginal parliamentary constituencies. The problem of pinning down a policy has led observers to conclude that there is 'no clear government policy on the desired shape of the DIB'[2] and that:

> current UK defence policy consists of neither a coherent interventionist philosophy with an articulated defence policy; nor a consistent enterprise policy, willing to rely on the beneficial effects of international market forces.[3]

This is a forceful but not unreasonable judgement. But even for leading arms-producing nations a full range of options for the procurement of large systems is unlikely to be available. Decisions, though erratic and appearing to lack continuity of objective, cannot always be otherwise.

The reasons for an absence of clearly articulated procurement policies are twofold. First, governments understandably like to keep a range of options open. Secondly, outright expressions of home preference can attract political and trade penalties when the tide of the times is against them and markets are becoming globalized. However, a preference for buying from home firms, on occasion rooted in sentiment and fertilized by nothing more than effective industrial lobbying, still pervades Alliance procurement policy. Roger Facer commented in 1975 that governments will only turn to 'collaboration' (which can take many forms), when the cost of proceeding otherwise is unsustainable or when the relevant technology is unavailable.[4] The maintenance of national capabilities has meant that 15 years later the scale of collaboration amongst the governments of major arms producers is still quite small. That is not necessarily a bad thing.

Governments' lack of enthusiasm for collaboration is shared by their industries. Open markets allow – indeed require – that firms compete rather than co-operate, if they are to work to allocate scarce resources effectively and maximize economic benefit. The managers of firms in reasonably uncontrolled markets understand this and seek to maximize the gains that the opportunity to compete allows. In consequence, as economists have noted,[5] inter-company co-operation becomes for the most part an arrangement of last resort which firms only enter into if they lack the financial or technical resources to carry a project through for themselves, or if the government, on which they rely for revenue, embroils them willy-nilly in a co-operative venture. Not only is the opportunity to optimize long-term profit lost by such arrangements but also, and of equal significance, a firm's competitive advantage may be eroded by giving rivals access to valuable technology which is then seized on and turned against it in the home market. The risks are obviously particularly extreme in high technology industries, where the initially stronger and dominant partner can be enfeebled or even have effective control wrested from him. The experience of the UK car-making group Austin Rover, which lost both market share and consumer credibility when it entered into a joint venture which led to Japanese Honda cars being sold under the prestigious Rover badge, is a case in point. But even if co-operation is unattractive, seeking to win business in a competitive market does not necessarily appeal, so long as there remains a third alternative of continuing to rely on government bias towards indigenous firms, provided that yields satisfactory profits. And for some of the state-owned or state-controlled defence firms in continental Europe, even profit may be either an irrelevant consideration or a problem susceptible to creative accounting.

This mutual interest in preserving established patterns of equipment buying means that change is slow in coming, and moves to explore other ways of buying will not be dramatic, except for low value items. Co-operation will continue to take second place. A good example of current political thinking on the topic can be found in the UK Labour Party's defence policy document drawn up in 1989. Although it contains a major change of party policy on nuclear weapons, there is nothing radical in what it has to say about procurement policy and the defence industries. Having said that, the government 'must get proper value for the public money that will continue to be spent on procurement from [UK] industries', and pointed out that 'R&D for the defence industries must not be allowed to displace essential R&D in successful and job-creating manufacturing industry', it goes on:

> We must ensure that material and equipment are obtained from the most sensible source. *A Buy British Policy will be adopted as a firm rule*, with appropriate exceptions where these make sense. We must, in addition, participate in joint ventures with our European partners in the Alliance. While a US contribution will continue, it is essential

to retain and safeguard a European procurement capability (emphasis added).[6]

Though there might be some quibbling over the fact that defence firms are themselves manufacturers and therefore create and sustain jobs, this is a manifesto which, with appropriate substitutions, would serve for almost any Alliance government.

Despite its leaning towards immobility, the reference in the text to joint ventures is a reminder that policy can develop when the financial shoe starts to pinch. Staying with the UK example, a pattern of aerospace procurement emerges which starts with self-sufficiency in the 1950s, develops into shared production with the US in the 1960s because of rising unit costs, swings towards collaboration with European partners in the 1970s because of budget pressures now coupled with fears of loss of national capability, and turns in the 1980s to placing greater reliance on market forces to drive prices down. For this latest approach to yield maximum benefits, national markets must be opened, though not unregulated, and foreign equipment, from whatever source, evaluated on all relevant dimensions in fair competition with home production. The development from stage to stage so far has not been clear-cut, has certainly not been consistent and is not yet complete. For example, emergent new producers are coming up with new competitive challenges. Although the rate and pattern of change differs from country to country and from one equipment area to another, significant developments have occurred. These can be expected to continue.

Policy options
Large scale procurement choices have in the past been made from the following basic options, some of which have sub-variants. They are the nationalist policy of purchase from indigenous industry; home production under license or through sharing in the manufacture of equipment developed abroad; international collaboration in development and production, or in production alone, which can be organized in a variety of ways; and, lastly, buying competitively from overseas. The distinctions are most marked at the finished product level, but they are not absolute because of manufacturers' reliance on foreign sourcing of components and sub-systems whichever way trade flows. Some indication of the scale of mutual reliance can be obtained from a current example in the civil aircraft field, where in a particular category there are two directly competing products. The 'British' aircraft has a 48% UK content by value. Its 'foreign' competitor is 52% British. Which one should the respective governments promote? Moreover, the 'foreignness' of a piece of equipment can be minimized by switching components if this makes the product more attractive. Even in the US arms industry, import penetration at the component and sub-assembly level reached 19% in 1986.[7]

48

As if this did not make choice difficult enough, national procurement can be either competitive or non-competitive, even at the finished product level, if there is more than one supplier. And in any of the buying modes it can be in the interest of both buyer and seller to introduce the maximum amount of competition when sub-contracts are let. These can account for more than 70% of the cost of the finished product.

Even if the political, economic, social and industrial factors influencing procurement decisions could be set aside (which they cannot), a last overlay of complexity is given to hard choices by the fact that the interplay between the more operationally relevant considerations of performance, technical risk, availability and cost alter at different stages of the procurement cycle, which should encompass up-dating and modifying the equipment after it has entered service, as well as repair and maintenance. On this basis the procurement cycle can easily last for 35 years.

Decisions on which elements to count in the life-cycle of a piece of equipment and which to exclude can make it 'as long as a piece of string'. Basic research in particular fields, not directed towards specific equipment applications, may be carried out for many years before a requirement emerges which would not be feasible had the research work not been done. The procurement route chosen, for example buying 'off-the-shelf', can make some parts of the cycle irrelevant to an individual purchaser. However, in conceptual terms, an item of equipment which has to be specially produced to meet a specified requirement goes through five stages of creation. The first is a study of its feasibility. The second defines the project in terms of technical risk and seeks to estimate its eventual development and production cost. The third stage is development during which the equipment is designed, prototypes are built and individual sub-systems, supplied to the prime contractor from many different sources (including, on occasion, the customer), are integrated and made to work together. The latter task can be a difficult one with elaborate equipment involving a welter of electronic 'black boxes'. The production stage comes next and the final one is the support of the equipment in service. Sub-phases of development are common in expensive programmes.

The timescale for each of these phases varies enormously. A feasibility study can take only a few months, while development of a complex system can take ten years and production as long again. In-service life can then be planned for 15 years, and more often than not in practice extended beyond that. The pattern of a representative procurement cycle is outlined in Chart I at p. 50.

Proper project management requires that the steps are kept as separate as possible in terms of engineering progress, although advance orders may need to be placed for items and materials with long lead times. Decisions to proceed to the next stage should be taken only after

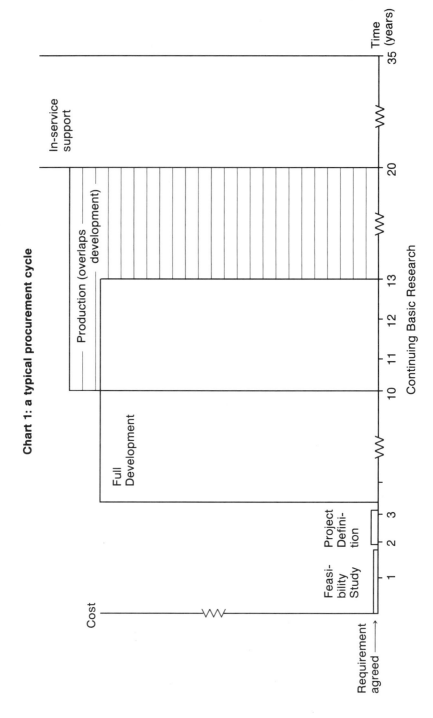

Chart 1: a typical procurement cycle

careful assessment of findings and progress. Failure to do this has led to extremely expensive fiascos. However, the discipline is by no means easy to maintain, especially when large sums have already been spent, deadlines have been missed and operational demands loom. Overlaps, especially between development and production are therefore frequent, and in the case of complex systems, inevitable. Sophisticated systems are being further developed throughout their life.

The early study phases absorb only a small proportion of the total cost of a project. A feasibility study, even for an ambitious requirement, might cost only $200,000. In contrast, the development cost of such a system, even if it is shared between nations, can lead to a bill of $2 bn for each country (the UK's share of EFA's development cost is $3.2 bn) and much more in complex US programmes. If only small quantities are then required or affordable, (and the quantities of each type of major equipment ordered by European nations in particular are moving steadily downwards), the ratio of cost between development and production can be as high as or even exceed 1:1, which generates concern about rising development costs as systems grow in complexity. The best known current example is the US B-2 stealth bomber, which is planned to be built in very small numbers, but which has a reported unit cost of $560 m.[8] Hence the long-standing concern of all arms makers, especially those in Europe, to increase production runs. But even if this could be done, the high absolute cost of developing military equipment resulting from the desire to exploit 'leading edge' technology remains. And equipment that is costly to develop and produce often means that very large capital sums have to be spent on more equipment to service it and keep it functioning in service. For example, the work necessary to design and build automatic test equipment for combat aircraft involves major development programmes in their own right.

In addition, the cost of keeping equipment in service for its useful life can exceed its initial procurement cost, while equipment that is cheap to buy may not be cheap to operate. These and other aspects of the cost of ownership now feature widely in procurement decisions. For example, 'spend to save' measures like designing-in better reliability and maintainability are now being recognized as cost-effective. Notwithstanding improvements of this kind, the cost of buying and using military equipment is high and will continue to grow.

Buying at home
Enough has been said about the military and industrial benefits of buying domestically to show that the strength of the arguments varies from case to case and that it is comparatively rare for the issue to be clear cut. The hard facts needed to show for certain whether for a particular item the benefits of supporting the home market outweigh any extra costs which might be incurred, are all too often not available. It is this which allows governments to avoid the need to face up to the cen-

tral issue of what indigenous industrial capacity it is sensible to keep. And because this central question is not answered, *ad hoc* decisions can be taken, sometimes of dubious validity, whenever choices come to be made about buying at home or buying abroad. The weight attached to each of the more easily varied factors in the equation – performance, risk, timescales, civil spin-off, sales potential, life cycle costs – can be almost subconsciously manipulated to give the answer that decision-makers want. There are no general guiding principles, only a traditional and widely shared wish to buy nationally if at all possible. Nor is that preference confined to governments. Procurement staff, for understandable reasons, prefer to do business with familiar firms. Buying complex things from foreigners at a distance is not the easiest way of working.

For less complex and therefore less expensive items requiring little development, a policy of home preference is unlikely to be costly. Similar pieces of equipment will be available from abroad and it is easy to check that the prices paid at home are not drifting away from those prevailing in world markets. It may even be possible to select through competition in the home market. National procurement does not necessarily mean higher prices.

The difficult choices arise where there is a complex new requirement to be met. Almost by definition there will only be a single national firm capable of undertaking the contract if a new platform is involved, and it will not have a suitable item on the shelf. A costly and lengthy development programme will be necessary, which the customer must fund, carrying high technical risk. The firm may then become highly dependent on the project, making it difficult to cancel when problems arise. The UK's national *Nimrod* AEW project at the time of its cancellation, after nine years of development at a cost in excess of $1.3 bn, was already four years behind its planned entry into service for training. Although in such cases it may be possible to limit the scope for cost growth during development by contracting on a fixed price basis (if the firm can be persuaded to agree), even the main theoretical attraction of a rigid policy of national procurement – namely that the equipment, when it is finally produced, should come very close to meeting the national requirement – is not always achieved in practice. In any case, with 20-year development and production timescales, it is something of an act of faith to believe that the people who lay down the requirement are sufficiently prescient to know the exact nature of the threat the equipment will be needed to counter. Revision of the requirement during the development phase to meet a revised threat assessment is not uncommon, but has obvious penalties for both costs and timescale. But, generally, the lengthened procurement cycle, and the fact that rising costs mean that fewer units can be afforded, oblige specifiers to call for performance which covers all the options, thereby stretching the technology, and/or to budget for performance updates.

For a nation to bear alone expensive development programmes, accept the risks inherent in early commitment to new technology and pay costs that may not derive in full from market pressures, is to put a high price on the maintenance of indigenous defence industrial capability. The trends examined earlier suggest that even France and the US are finding that price too high. The difficulty is that there is no easy way of comparing the aggregated cost of continuing with present policies with their alternatives. And even if governments form a clear vision of what they want their national DIBs to look like, there is still the question of whether any necessary restructuring should be initiated and managed through protection, subsidies and the use of government contracts as an instrument of policy, or whether an optimum industrial structure will be the end result of allowing market forces to operate. Although France has, with some success, followed the former course, it is still left with over-capacity in both its public and private defence industrial sectors as its export markets have contracted. In the US and the UK there has been greater willingness to allow commercial pressures to precipitate change, both in declining heavy industries and new high-tech industries generally considered to be vital to the future health of any developed economy. In none of the major arms producing countries, however, have the defence industries been fully exposed to the effects of an open market: effects which may energize some firms but terminally debilitate others.

Licensed or co-production
The advantages of using domestic industry to make another country's equipment, whether wholly or in part, are principally the saving of R&D costs and the creation or maintenance of employment in the customer nation. There should also be some transfer of technology to the buyer's industry, though its further use may be restricted. There are three basic production routes which can be adopted: straightforward production under license solely to satisfy the buyer's requirements, co-production in which each nation participates in the total production of both nations' requirements and exports, and a third work-sharing variant in which the buyer is given some of the work on his own order.

European purchase of a great deal of US equipment has to date been on the basis of licensed production. It appeals particularly to small nations who have neither the resources nor the ambition to develop advanced systems for themselves. And it is attractive to the US government and industry, who see licensed production as second-best to outright export sales but preferable to joint ventures involving shared development because it is possible to control access to technology. NATO has always favoured licensed production because it contributes to standardization and interoperability.

Delaying commitment to new equipment until it can be seen to be in production and working has obvious attractions to buyers. However, licensed production is not without its limitations. It is only worthwhile paying to duplicate production facilities if quantities are large and economies of scale can be obtained. In addition the buyer usually has to pay a development levy, although this will normally be only a small part of the development cost. Moreover the customer may still be obliged to rely on the exporter to supply vital sub-systems. The technology gain may therefore be limited. Design changes and modifications are also inevitable as the buyer sets about 'customizing' the equipment. Finally, on the negative side of the balance sheet in the case of European co-operation with US firms, is the issue of the exportability of the resulting product to third countries. Even though the licensed co-production partner may be willing to export any technology he may have contributed to the project, the probability that the US government or its contractors will restrict the sale of the complete weapon system for perceived political, economic and/or military reasons, makes European nations wary. After all, achieving the economies of scale of large production runs not only through pooling the collaborators' requirements but also by selling abroad, is a basic reason for joint production.

When these factors are taken together with the innumerable minor inefficiencies caused by problems of language, technical interpretation and management, licensed production leads to higher costs for the same item than direct importation. A much quoted example, which bears further repetition, is the four-nation European co-production of the F-16 combat aircraft, where the customers paid 34% more for the aircraft than would have been the cost of direct purchase from the US.[9] No doubt the customers took the view that the benefits they enjoyed in terms of jobs, offset sales, technology transfer and so on were worth more than this cost premium. For the exporter it was either a matter of transferring work, in this case 58% of the dollar value of the European governments' order, or no sale. Rather than endure cost penalties of this order, the larger European nations, with capable industries and a technological base to sustain, have turned to collaborating amongst themselves, pooling resources jointly to develop and produce advanced equipment. Licensed production is no longer in vogue.

International collaboration

International collaboration is most marked in the aerospace sector where, in Europe, complexity and cost mean that development of a new system is certain to be done internationally. If past and present projects are included, there have already been 13 multinational military aerospace programmes in Europe, seven of which have been helicopter projects.[10]

The simplest form of international collaboration involves nations agreeing separately to develop related weapons and then to buy from each other. Since the 1960s, when France and the UK pioneered a joint helicopter programme, discussion has centred on sharing projects between the US and Europe, but only the AMRAAM/ASRAAM family of advanced medium- and short-range air-to-air missiles has got beyond the talk stage. Even then, AMRAAM, which is being developed nationally by the US, has run into difficulties, while Germany and the UK, who set out to develop ASRAAM together, are no longer doing so.

This approach minimizes but does not eliminate the problems of agreeing on requirements, and it makes for simple project organization. There are also no balance of payments penalties during development. However, the track record is poor and it will in any case remain an approach that can only be used occasionally because of the difficulties in grouping requirements.

EUROPEAN COLLABORATION
The central economic argument which has driven joint development and production in Europe is that savings are obtained from shared R&D and longer production runs, even though the absolute R&D cost is higher than that of a purely national programme. The scale of the R&D premium is a matter of some debate. Its size depends on the complexity of the project, the number, efficiency and technical competence of the partner nations, their previous experience of collaboration and the willingness of the firms involved to work together. Although the key determinant of cost is 'How much do we already know in relation to where we want to get?', factors like the compatibility of management styles and readiness to share information are often given insufficient weight when a balance of advantage between proceeding nationally or collaboratively comes to be struck.

It is therefore only to be expected that when alternative procurement routes have to be evaluated in theory rather than practice, the collaborative R&D cost premium is a matter for some speculation, even for a given project with known variables. However, collaborative projects are almost by definition expensive, and therefore if there is a price premium, the baseline will be high. Although the collaborative database is slender, conventional wisdom has it that costs increase by between 30 and 50% for each additional partner.[11] And clearly the more partners there are, the less the benefit to each.

As far as production cost savings are concerned, even combining orders from European countries tends to yield a smaller total than many US production runs. This, together with the established (but wasteful) pattern of each participant having its own final assembly lines means that benefits of scale are restricted. The gains from improvement in operator performance through practice – the 'learner' effect, which in aircraft production, for example, is mainly confined to the construction of the airframe, accounting for less than half the cost of the finished product – are also limited. Empirical evidence suggests that they are in any case smaller in Europe than in the US. The average saving on unit cost is about 5% for each doubling of the number made.

And, in the final analysis, the cost savings to be obtained from learning are only as large as the contract with the manufacturer lays down. Even so, in theory, there should be some production cost savings. In practice they are almost invariably cancelled out by the complexity of equipment which, within one weapon system, has to satisfy a number of separate operational requirements. For example, the mass of the *Tornado* aircraft increased by over 50% from that originally planned when the UK joined the project. And increased mass equals increased cost. Equipment produced collaboratively will tend either to have some features that are not required by all the users or, because of conflicting performance demands, fall short of everybody's needs in some or other way.

It therefore has to be asked whether the inefficiencies associated with collaboration are any longer affordable. In reaching judgements, enthusiastic supporters of this form of European co-operation feel that they can legitimately lift their heads from the profit and loss accounts and pay it in aid as a device for combating the threat of technological dominance by the US and Japan and the consequent reduction of European firms to sub-contractor status. Collaboration, they argue, even if it has a cost, allows Europe to compete internationally, preserves industrial capacity and jobs, and prevents a US monopoly. More cynically, both defence firms and their customers know that collaborative projects are relatively immune from cancellation once they are into development.

Although it has never been suggested that these benefits are wholly illusory or that they are lacking in value, it is practically impossible to quantify the gains that they produce and thus reach an objective assessment of costs and benefits. More easily measurable are the savings which can be made when countries and industries collaborate in R&D, thereby avoiding duplication of effort. Standardization of equipment, setting aside its military merits, is another clear-cut benefit which collaboration brings. Through sharing the cost of training and logistic support, collaborative European projects have also enjoyed major export successes.

The remaining benefits which collaboration is said to bring are altogether more vague. However, it seems reasonable to assume that sharing technical knowledge, and the inevitable rivalry between engineers that goes with this, results in a better product. At the very least, the technological and industrial competence of the weaker partners is brought closer to that of the stronger. Whether this is either an economically or commercially desirable proposition depends on the observer's standpoint. Finally, there is the intangible contribution that nations working together at the forefront of technology is said to bring to political relationships and Alliance cohesion. The available evidence surrounding this notion is inconclusive, and likely to remain so.

The difficulties that have been experienced in joint arms ventures, despite the economic and technical logic which lay behind them, are inevitable when proud, powerful, protectionist and economically competitive states, with similar industrial capabilities, try to work harmoniously together. Clashes are inevitable as firms and governments seek, almost unconsciously, to dominate their rivals-cum-partners. There is no technological imperative or military motive to prevent it. Collaboration works best when there are complementary asymmetries in national capabilities and goals – asymmetries which may have to be sustained for many years. But major inequalities do not exist amongst the leading nations, and second division players have aspirations to join the premier league. Submissive government partners and their industrial proxies are in short supply. For these reasons alone, the future prospects for successful European joint ventures between governments must be severely limited unless and until national DIBs are rationalized, and nation states show by example rather than words that they are engaging in arms production with the prime objective of fostering European integration rather than maximizing national advantage.

Meanwhile, the landscape of European collaboration is littered with examples of irreparable, stalled or barely-moving projects with the inability to decide on and stick to a common design as the common cause of their difficulties or downfall. For example, the UK's House of Commons Defence Committee recently said that progress on the third generation anti-tank missile was 'far from satisfactory', because it had taken seven years to agree the requirement with France and Germany.[12] The Franco-German PAH-2 anti-tank helicopter project has also been bedevilled by disagreements over the design, and the project nearly foundered. The original conception of a single design to meet each partner's requirement has now been split into two different variants, Germany buying one and France buying both.

Many other examples could be given, but it is EFA that has been described as 'perhaps the best example of requirement disharmony'.[13] Three nations, the UK, France and Germany, initiated the project in 1979. By 1983, when the European Staff Target was agreed, Spain and Italy had joined. However, the variation in national requirements was considerable and the partners could not agree on a final design or work-sharing arrangements. The French decision to proceed alone with *Rafale* and the consequent Spanish vacillation meant that full development did not start until late 1988. Even in early 1990, after three changes of name and several changes of partners, the project is not completely secure. Both West Germany and Italy are reported to have insufficient cash to continue to participate in the project,[14] and protracted difficulties in agreeing on the radar to be selected suggests that EFA will run late. And, although not directly a consequence of the collaborative nature of the project, both Germany and the UK, the major partners, seem likely in the end to reduce their planned buys, thus increasing unit production costs.

On the general question of delay in collaborative projects, whether or not they invariably take longer than national projects depends on the point at which the clock is started. If the time taken to harmonize requirements is included, the evidence is that collaborative projects take longer, even allowing for the fact that they are always complex and there is only a limited field for comparison. However, if the time-scale is taken as the period from the start of development to the completion of production, the picture looks brighter. One academic author has concluded that there is 'no evidence that joint ventures take longer to develop than other European national projects'.[15] The limited history of collaborative efforts and the wide difference between types of project make it impossible to reach firm conclusions beyond the obvious one that the more complex the programme, the more likely it is to be delayed and therefore to cost more. Furthermore, the more partners there are, the greater the difficulties of getting all the runners to the starting gate at the same time with parliamentary and financial approvals intact, and the greater the probability that at some stage in the project one or other of them will run short of money or change their equipment priorities, thereby causing the programme to be stretched. It is perhaps significant that the reason given by the US for its withdrawal from the now-defunct eight nation collaborative NFR90 NATO Frigate programme, announced in October 1989, was the time taken and the limited prospects for achieving a common design.[16]

At the industrial level, the leaching of technology from the more expert firms to the less proficient, which collaboration inevitably involves, leaves the former torn between the loss of competitive advantage and the loss of work if they decline to join collaborative projects – assuming they have the option. There were, however, few complaints when EFA development contracts worth $10 bn were placed without the benefit of competition at the prime contractor level.

The inefficiencies that arise in collaborative projects through the compromises which emerge from wrangling over the terms of the inter-governmental Memoranda of Understanding (MOU) which are their rule book, and their organizational complexity, though not of the same order, should not be ignored. Even administration costs are high on large international programmes. It has been estimated that they added 1.6% to the *Tornado* project costs.[17]

However, it is the occasionally baroque and generally fragmented decision-making processes common in such programmes, in which the quality of the decision is governed by the need for consensus and agreement by junior partners on issues affecting the major players before action can be taken, which introduce more serious but unfortunately unquantifiable penalties. In the case of the SP 70 tri-national howitzer, which started development in 1973, after much delay, and finally petered out in 1986 with nothing to show, the absence of firm central management arrangements and taut contracts were held largely to blame. The problem is minimized if a single contractor is nominated to manage the project on behalf of all the nations. However, this requires both in theory and in practice that one nation and its industry are acknowledged as leading the venture. The political problems this creates have led collaborative projects increasingly to be managed through joint venture companies and supervised by an international management agency, each with their own bureaucracies. As if this did not make the structure top-heavy enough, the high political profile of the large projects (the production phase of *Tornado* involved 500 firms and 70,000 employees), means that each nation's military, civilian and technical procurement staff cannot bring themselves to stand back from day-to-day management and resist the temptation to meddle in the affairs of the international brokers and their own industry. There are careers to be pursued, and collaborative projects offer more opportunities to shine than many others. More layers are therefore added to an overblown management superstructure until, on occasion, for every person properly described as a project manager there are a number of pretenders to the role. There have even been examples of ambassadors becoming deeply involved in collaborative negotiations because of the perceived international relations dimension. It is no wonder that a UK Parliamentary Committee concluded in 1988 that 'the current arrangements adopted in many collaborative programmes are unsatisfactory in several respects'.[18] Some of the problems of collaboration are illustrated in the two brief project descriptions which follow.

EH101
In certain cases, the byzantine structure of collaborative projects can seem almost wilful. The Anglo/Italian EH101 project, for example, although in its main military variant intended to be an ASW aircraft for the Royal Navy and the Italian Navy, is planned in addition to have military and civil transport versions deriving from a common design. The resulting 'integrated' programme is funded jointly by the two MODs and the two nations' manufacturers (Westland and Agusta), supported by launch funding from the two industry departments. A joint venture company, wholly owned by the firms on which the main development contract is let, is intended to supervise its owners. In addition, the two MODs have separate national development contracts with other companies for their respective (and different) avionics systems, which will be supplied to the main development contractor for integration into the weapons-platform. The massive management problems of allocation of effort and control between the two nations to which such an arrangement gives rise, where no single contractor has responsibility for system performance, can readily be imagined. The fact that budgetary pressures led to such an arrangement does not excuse its creation.

The joint staff target for the EH101 was agreed in 1979. Ten years on, and six years into development, the programme, which would at current prices cost the UK more than $2.5 bn for 50 aircraft, even though the development cost is shared equally with Italy, is experiencing difficulties. Substantial time and development cost overruns, in a project where the development to production cost ratio is already 1:1, are certain. The aircraft is likely to be five years late in entering service. This is not solely attributable to the fact that it is a collaborative project. But the organizational complexity which collaboration demanded, and the failure of UK and Italian industry to work harmoniously together, accounts for much of what has gone wrong. It is a far cry from the claim made by the two nations' NADs that 'through collaboration we have a cost-effective programme and are seeking to strengthen our industrial base'[19], and it indicates clearly that the price of collaboration can sometimes be too high. The UK is now reconsidering its planned order for the military transport version.[20]

By no means do all collaborative projects have such a dismal history. Lessons are being learned, and no doubt if the EH101 project was initiated today it would be structured very differently. However, even in the very latest and smartest programme, EFA, closely modelled on *Tornado*, there is room for improvement.

EFA
The EFA project improves on *Tornado* in a number of ways. There will be no national variants: all the partners only want an agile fighter. The development contract was let on the basis of a detailed specification, and it provides for payment only when specific milestones are achieved. The potential for funding imbalances to develop has been removed and work-shares will not be adjusted retrospectively. Good prices for equipment have been obtained through competition. The aircraft's radar, which will account for about 20% of its unit cost, will also be bought competitively.

On the other hand, the main contract was not let competitively and some of the development work is not yet subject to a maximum price limitation. Moreover, there is no single contractor with overall responsibility for the project. Separate consortia are developing the airframe and the engine. No firm commitments have been made to the production quantities on which the financial case for the project rests, in part because it has been acknowledged that some areas of technical risk remain. It has been estimated that over the whole life of the project, including the in-service phase, the UK's requirements will be met for only 5% less than the cost of a national programme. This is against a background in which Parliament's Comptroller and Auditor General reported, after examining ten previous collaborative projects, that 'the study found it hard to evaluate the extent of any financial and other benefits actually accruing from collaboration'.[21]

EFA might be expected to cost $30 m each at 1989 prices – perhaps half as much again as similar aircraft which are now flying. With such uncertainties about the savings generated by established modes of collaboration, and in the light of their pitfalls, there seems to be a very strong case for maximizing competition within collaborative projects at the sub-contract level and promoting the thought that direct competition amongst prime contractors might produce further savings.

TRANSATLANTIC COLLABORATION

Although it is economic necessity that has driven the European nations to collaborate, France and Germany are unequivocal in considering the contribution which successful large-scale projects make to European political and industrial strength and cohesion as a clear subsidiary benefit. The UK has been ambivalent about such factors, fearing the consequences for the already debilitated 'special relationship' with the US and the loss of industrial access to US technology if it became too enthusiastic about Europe. Thus, there was considerable surprise when the then Minister of Defence, Michael Heseltine, strove vigorously, but in the end unavailingly, for a European solution to the problem of rescuing the ailing UK helicopter company, Westland. However, despite the differences in size of US and European firms, problems of technology transfer and, in the case of France, political as well as geographical distancing, none of the Europeans have turned away from America entirely. The US, for its part, mindful of the political stresses caused by the transatlantic arms trade imbalance, and needing access to European markets, has steadily put machinery in place designed to facilitate the growth of bilateral and multilateral projects between Europe and the US.

Transatlantic collaboration is more limited than that between the European nations and has not in the main followed the European pattern. There is therefore scope for developing innovative forms of collaboration and the US Administration now insists that every defence acquisition project is assessed for its co-operative potential. Furthermore, under the DOD's International Materiel Evaluation scheme and NATO's Comparative Test Programme, the US military are committed to evaluate foreign weapons and systems with the aim of avoiding procurements which re-invent the wheel. In 1989, 32 items, predominantly European in origin, were evaluated.

The number of co-operative development or 'Nunn Amendment' projects funded from that part of the US equipment budget fenced-off for spending in joint-funded projects with one or more European nations is also increasing. More than a dozen new projects were started in 1988, spanning a wide range of technologies from laser weapons applications and counter-measures, through combat vehicle command and control systems to aircraft shelter upgrades.

Both customers and contractors have an interest in fostering arrangements of this kind. For the military, transatlantic programmes share a key attraction of their European counterparts – the political capital invested in them makes them less vulnerable to cutback or cancellation. Industry also recognizes this attraction but, in contrast to European ventures founded on *juste retour*, both US and European industry see Nunn projects as potential vehicles for gaining market access. From the US viewpoint this is a big plus point as 1992 approaches. Transatlantic co-operation can therefore be expected to increase, although its potential will still be constrained by restrictive US policies on exports and technology transfer. Moreover, if the taxpayer is to get maximum value for money it will be important to ensure that it does not develop in a manner which impedes competition.

Competition
Although it is accepted that there are occasions and circumstances when, even in narrow economic terms, the market mechanism works imperfectly, economic theory and empirical evidence suggest that customers buy in non-competitive markets at their peril. *Ceteris paribus*, competition spurs efficiency, alters attitudes and lowers prices. The belated recognition that this is a universal economic truth which can hold good even in the 'different' defence market has proved a much needed stimulant to change, although it remains to be seen whether competition in defence procurement is here to stay or will simply be a short, sharp shock.

Seeking competitive bids to satisfy an equipment requirement is only part of a package of measures which Alliance nations are now, to varying degrees, adopting to bring a more commercial approach to all aspects of the procurement process. In addition to competitive international bidding itself, at both development and production stages fixed price contracts are negotiated in place of cost-plus arrangements; progress payments on large projects, which ran at 90–95% are now reduced to 70% and tied to measurable technical advances; and bidding against 'cardinal points' specifications, which set out the performance required in general terms rather than obsessive detail, thereby encouraging an innovative response, is encouraged. Firmly settling project responsibility on a single contractor is another important feature of the policy.

There are as yet no spectacular results from this policy. The pressure on profit margins which a more commercial approach to procurement might have been expected to exercise has not yet of itself set in train significant restructuring of an overcrowded industry. The restructuring that is occurring is largely in anticipation of hard times ahead. Moreover, the savings that competition has yielded have proved hard to identify. The UK has set a target for savings through competition totalling some $1.2 bn over a five-year period[22] – not a dramatically large sum, but there is no reliable way of knowing whether it will be achieved, or at any rate achieved through competitive procurement. It is only possible to compare the price actually paid with an estimate of what might have been paid in the absence of competition, which makes it all too easy to obtain the answer that is wanted.

It is not necessary to look far for the reasons why competition policy has so far had only a minimal effect on profits. First, defence dependency amongst the major suppliers is very variable. Secondly, in 1987–8 only half the UK's defence contracts were let on the basis of some form of competition, a fall from 64% two years earlier, and contracts for 90% of equipment expenditure by value are still awarded to UK companies.[23] Officials justify this on the arguably optimistic and certainly unproven grounds that it is 'overwhelmingly because British companies are able to offer value for money'.[24] This suggests that there is room for more rigorous application of competition, including buying from abroad, provided both customer and supplier play the competition game fairly. Competition must be internationalized if it is to bring maximum benefit. Artificial preservation of the capacity for domestic competition is not a viable option when, as now, fewer orders introduce discontinuities into production. The alternative of always buying from a single national contractor is even less palatable.

The almost undented financial performance of major contractors, which may in part be accounted for by increased efficiency as a consequence of competition, indicates that it is important to ensure that fixed price competitive bidding really does save money. Fixed prices can preserve or even increase margins compared to cost-plus contracts if sufficient contingency against technical risk is built into the price, and contractors negotiate prices which minimize their financial exposure. In one notorious example, 60% of the contract value was revealed to be contingency.[25] Naturally there will be occasions when the contractor has to spend this contingency. The fixed price trade-off is between a 'competitive' price and the contractor footing the bill when things go wrong. But in practice, if a contractor runs into serious financial difficulty because of problems on a fixed price contract, the operational need for the equipment may well mean that the fixed price will be renegotiated. In the US there is already some concern over the cost of competitive fixed price contracts and orders are again being placed on a cost-plus basis. If contractors will not accept the high technical or financial risks common in defence contracts, or take measures to insulate themselves from them, a competitive approach to procurement will not produce the lowest possible price for equipment which meets the specification. Moreover, when competition does operate to squeeze margins, repeated doses may drive firms from the market, thereby limiting the scope for domestic competition and ultimately restricting or even destroying international competition.

Industrialists point to other drawbacks. For example, the sheer cost of bidding to meet complex specifications and satisfy elaborate bidding procedures, with levels of transparency which vary from country to country, can make firms think twice about tendering if they judge their chances of success to be low. This is more likely to be a consideration for small or medium-sized firms; the potential winners of big contracts have no option but to join the only game in town. But it can be an expensive game to play. One UK equipment firm has spent a seven-figure sum in preparing its bid for a new contract.[26] And costs can spiral if the customer engages in several rounds of competitive tendering in an effort to drive prices down – a process which can result in illusory savings if initial prices are set in the expectation of further rounds of tendering.

Repeated tendering, together with the time taken to analyse bids, means that relying on competition often extends already protracted procurement processes by many months. Further delay can be introduced when there is separate bidding for development and production, and even for separate production batches. Not only do the bidding processes take time, but contract negotiations are drawn out because of quite understandable disputes about the ownership of 'intellectual property'. This is a thorny enough issue when it is confined to argument about whether the expertise needed to create a piece of equipment was generated by commercial or government funding, and therefore which party owns the intellectual property and has the right to use it, but the problems are compounded when a company faces the prospect of a competitor being given access to technical know-how. And, to add insult to injury, delays can erode the profit margin in a fixed price bid unprotected from inflation as time passes.

Uncertainty about winning production orders also makes firms cautious about investing in 'private venture' R&D, thus limiting innovation and design effectiveness. The damage is potentially serious among firms developing specialized components which may be incorporated in a weapons system five or even ten years after the technology was pioneered. Capital investment to improve production efficiency and so reduce costs and prices will also be cut in conditions of uncertainty.

For a policy of competition to produce the greatest gains, there must be new procedures and new attitudes in entrenched bureaucracies as well as a political willingness to allow market forces to work. Even now, when such competition as there is in defence markets leads a government to conclude that it should buy expensive items from abroad, there is an automatic requirement for the cost, or more than the cost, to be 'offset' by the supplier through purchases from the customer country. This may involve undertaking to place work on the contract with the buyer's industry, entering into a commitment to buy comparable, invariably high-tech items from the customer, or some other form of counter-trade. Offset arrangements often involve a combination of all of these. The net effect is that it costs the seller more to produce, and either his profit is cut or the buyer pays more than he need. When the offset commitment is higher than the value of the contract, for example in the case of the French and British purchase of AWACS aircraft where the manufacturer, Boeing, undertook to offset the value of the order by 130%, these hidden costs are multiplied. And, of course, if the offset arrangement does not involve the customer winning the offset business on the basis of fair competition, the position is no better than that which obtains under *juste retour*. Governments are not immune from a natural tendency to prefer existing ways of doing business.

However, despite the weaknesses associated with or even endemic in a policy of competitive arms procurement, firms where it has been tried have generally welcomed it. It is the prospect of profit which tips the scales. Efficient managers, through tight control of costs and commercially astute contract negotiation, can maximize margins on domestic contracts. The productivity gains also allow more competitive prices to be quoted abroad. And taxpayers need have no worries if profits are high but prices are low.

IV. THE PROSPECTS FOR PROGRESS

The limitations of the established collaborative models and the cultural and political difficulties of forming new groupings, or even perpetuating existing ones, suggest that this form of European joint procurement may not grow much beyond its present relatively modest levels, despite the continued shrinkage of equipment budgets. François Heisbourg has observed that 'the heyday of co-operation is behind us'.[1] Without undue pedantry, it would be more true to say that while the heyday of *collaboration* is over, the pressures to find new ways of increasing *co-operation*, whilst benefitting from competition, are still very much with us.

For example, there is a well established but now vital need for government agencies and firms to co-operate internationally in research, however loath they may be to do so. Modest, and in some cases declining, research budgets in both the public and private sectors must be pooled if companies are to survive to meet future military demands. The reluctance of private European firms to invest, innovate and exploit, caused by their extended protection from international competition, has left them exposed to the consequences of the IEPG's plan to open the market at a time of diminishing defence expenditure. To survive, European firms and governments will have to share their knowledge and build up a European critical mass in high cost high-tech activity. There is no longer room for competition in research in Europe, especially if firms are to cover the areas of technology, such as stealth, where the US will want to keep its knowledge to itself. Moreover, it is becoming increasingly important for civil and military divisions within companies to share technical knowledge because of the growing overlap in the civil and military applications of technology.

Sharing between firms makes for greater freedom and openness in looking at whole markets and provides the opportunity for a joint market assault when competitive advantage can be gained, as well as focusing attention on joint co-operative opportunities. However, knowledge should be shared in ways which do not involve the surrender of national capabilities at a basic level of research when the companies doing the sharing have an undoubted long-term commercial future. Moreover, although there is no clear distinction between 'pre-competitive' research and that associated with bringing specific products to the market, it is important that co-operative research does not lead to cartelization.

So far as the plethora of European programmes with tortuous acronyms (ESPRIT, BRITE, BAP, RACE, EUREKA) and so on are concerned, the Community's declared and repeated policy of maximizing competition at every opportunity goes a long way to ensure that these programmes, which are jointly funded by government and industry, with insistence on cross-border co-operation as the *quid pro quo* for public investment, do not lead to market distortion. In the case of inter-firm technology alliances and R&D agreements, some 500 of which had been identified by as long ago as 1985,[2] the public is unlikely to be so well protected, although managers in companies which are co-operating will always tend to have in mind the point at which firms could, involved with advantage, become competitors.

There is no shortage of models to be followed where public funding is involved. European Community funding of co-operative research runs at $1.5 bn annually, and nearly 70 such co-operative ventures are thought to exist, many of which involve a multitude of separate contracts.[3] For the co-operative European Technology Programme proposed by the IEPG, a French plan christened EUCLID (European Co-operative Long-term Initiative in Defence), following the model of the EC's civilian EUREKA programme, has been adopted.[4]

No decisions have been reached on how such a programme is to be jointly funded. The emphasis on the 'long-term' is probably a pointer. Nonetheless IEPG NADs are charged with developing 'firm plans' and ministers claim that funding could amount to $120 m in 1990.[5] However, the EUCLID model has been found wanting by the nine European aircraft manufacturing companies who, having shared with the Community the costs of a massive further study released in 1989, have proposed yet another co-operative research programme funded, as might be expected, by the Community.[6] Its aim is to increase combined research expenditure by 50–60% in five years to enable European industry to compete with the US. Pre-competitive 'upstream' programmes of this or the EUREKA/EUCLID types can clearly cut their participants' costs and minimize duplication. Despite the difficulties in making them work they are, therefore, to be encouraged. Furthermore, co-operation on basic technologies is not necessarily inimical to downstream competition in development and production.

However, the chances of realizing the IEPG's dream of a European-wide defence-related research programme geared to satisfy disparate national equipment needs and making use of different levels of research ability, with established funding, were negligible even before recent events in the Soviet Union and Eastern Europe, together with the prospect of substantial conventional arms reduction, made continued public support for high levels of defence expenditure unlikely. It now has to be seen whether the prospect of less research money will force the pooling of expenditure or whether national institutions will press for the whole of a smaller cake. Until things become clearer, it seems best for European defence research to start with national initiatives between two partners which, if the soil proves fertile, will blossom and proliferate. The current Anglo-French defence research work points the way forward. Initiated with an exchange between defence ministers, half-a-dozen or so specific areas have been selected as having co-operative potential. A technology demonstrator programme for an air interception radar to build on EFA's technology for its successor in the year 2000 and beyond is a typical example.

The cause of this coming together is quite simple: the two countries have run out of money at the same time and have been obliged to join in a pragmatic and flexible partnership. It is an approach which the FRG, also short of funds, has yet to come to grips with. Yet in the roll of forced alliances, penury probably features more often than plenitude as a motivator. With the French, FRG and UK governments apparently lacking enthusiasm for further large-scale investment in the Community's Framework Programme of technological R&D, in which the Community plays the role of policy-maker, further co-operative defence research in the near term seems likely to depend on opportunistic partnerships between national governments and between their respective industries. In this way, at the very least, the danger of governments being obliged to buy the fruits of the technology their firms develop is minimized.

1992

The establishment, by the end of 1992, of a single internal market in Europe will mark the completion of a process of reduction and elimination of tariff barriers which has already been under way for ten years. Five hundred market-creating measures have been identified by the EC, and as at early 1990, nearly 400 of them have so far been agreed by the national governments of the Community nations. However, many of the remaining measures, including the abolition of frontier controls, VAT harmonization and social legislation, although the latter is not critical to the creation of the market itself, are proving politically controversial. Further progress will therefore be slow and the Europe of 1992 will prove far less integrated and harmonized than the optimists claim. There is no machinery for agreeing some of the most desirable features of a common market, such as acceptance of common standards and taxation.

The almost complete failure to date of the EC's public purchasing policy illustrates the difficulties of achieving a competitive market in the member states. A Public Supplies Directive came into force in 1977, designed to open public supply to competition. It was intended to apply to all contracts with a value in excess of $300,000, and contracting bodies were required to advertise for bids in the Official Journal of the European Commission (OJEC). In practice, purchasers have largely ignored the Directive. Only 3% of eligible tenders have been published in the OJEC, and only a handful of these have led to cross-national contract awards.

The EC is taking action to improve this position and, as noted in Chapter 1, has a long-term objective of bringing defence procurement within the ambit of its public purchasing policy. However, the existing EC bureaucracy is too small for its role in this area and has no effective policing powers. The IEPG, which currently has the task of opening the defence market, can hardly be less successful in introducing competition than the EC has been in other areas of public procurement.

68

However, the EC's failure does indicate what a difficult task they have, and with Europe likely to remain for some years a Europe of national markets in which openness in government procurement progresses only slowly, it seems equally certain that defence will be bringing up the rear.

US INDUSTRY AND 1992

Although defence procurement is a laggard in the run-up to 1992, the vague references to security in the Single European Act, which commits member states to 'maintain the technological and industrial conditions necessary for their security', provoked widespread apprehension in the US, and served to focus American attention on the rationalization and concentration in European defence industry which was already taking place. Amongst industrialists, fears were of two main kinds. First, that the new, larger and more efficient European firms would be able to compete more effectively in the US home market. Secondly, that the economic prosperity generated by unfettered trade flows would enable Europe to turn the tables and pay the premium for a 'Buy European' policy, closing their market to American competition.

The worries on the first point may be justified, although there are many who would argue that a unified but unprotected European market will create easy pickings for US firms. However, present – let alone future – pressures on equipment budgets make it unlikely that a significant European price premium can be afforded. Moreover, for a variety of reasons and for a long time, the European defence establishment has been pro-Atlantic in its outlook. One of the reasons for this is that the US government's application of tough, even unreasonable, technology transfer and export licensing policies has left Europe heavily reliant on American technology – a position the IEPG is unlikely to alter for some years, even though the sudden need to support Eastern European economies may lead to some marginal relaxation of US policy.

The creation of a European defence market, notwithstanding frequent statements that US firms will not be excluded, must carry some risk that the transatlantic trade disputes, which are becoming more frequent in civil markets, will spread to defence. So long as the wish for national industrial independence, separate from a commitment to a European common market in arms, remains predominant, US firms will not find themselves shut out. But if this attitude changes, as this Paper has argued it should and must, US contractors will need to sharpen their competitiveness. In this situation there will be no room for using technology restrictions to protect US industrial competitiveness; such an effort would eventually prove self-defeating. It will be wiser for US firms to apply superior technology to win export orders, which in turn generate the research funds needed to maintain a technological lead, thus creating a virtuous circle. And in those areas where Europe has or can create its own advanced technologies, the temptation for the US to restrict the transfer of its own technology, strong though it undoubtedly will be, must equally be resisted.

It is too early to reach firm conclusions about what the nature of the internal market might be, and its implications for US defence companies. However, if it develops as planned, albeit considerably more slowly than some envisage, American firms will have to find new ways of doing business with Europe. Some have already started, and there is a growing realization that the traditional approaches of direct sales, licensing agreements and case-by-case teaming will not keep them close to their European counterparts, who increasingly see themselves as peers rather than licensees or sub-contractors.

For US industry the basic options are the establishment of a permanent presence or the formation of strategic alliances. Within the former, the choice lies between setting-up overseas manufacturing subsidiaries to benefit from lower internal barriers and win local acceptance through providing employment and paying taxes, and buying – or at least taking a stake in – European defence firms. An important factor governing investment decisions is whether the resulting business will be said by the EC to be 'European' and therefore eligible for the full benefits of club membership. Differences in market conditions and in corporate resources and styles mean that strategies will vary but, insofar as a common pattern can be discerned, it seems that US companies are most attracted to linking with European firms with local knowledge and an understanding of the intricacies of local procurement decisions. The higher-risk strategy of buying companies in what will remain for some time small and politically impenetrable markets does not appeal. US and European firms can, of course, come together in many different ways and have done so in the past. However, if US firms in Europe are not to find their positions weakened, the existing generally loose alliances will have to become much more structured and permanent, and cover the full business spectrum from research, through development and production, to follow-on logistic support. Confining that philosophy to individual projects may no longer be adequate.

Meanwhile, the dramatic restructuring of the US equipment market will continue, as firms with low levels of defence dependency seek to divest themselves of defence interests and others are sold. Chrysler is trying to sell its aerospace interests, as are companies as diverse as Honeywell and Kodak, while Ford Aerospace, valued at $1.5 bn a few years ago, is now expected to sell, if at all, for $600 m.[7]

EUROPEAN INDUSTRY AND 1992

The defence industries have not been isolated from the wave of acquisitions, mergers and strategic alliances sweeping across Europe as companies prepare for the more competitive environment of 1992, when the shrinking budgets and over-capacity which have been discussed earlier in this Paper will leave contractors, and more particularly their sub-contractors, exposed. In this situation, as with US companies, the reaction will depend on market circumstances. Smaller companies confined to national markets may absorb others or be absorbed themselves when the need to obtain the critical mass necessary to face down competition is paramount. But there is growing evidence that both medium and large companies see advantage in the vertical integration which has been such a feature of the rationalization of the US industrial scene. The logic that is causing US airframe manufacturers to form links with European electronics companies could cause the same thing to happen in Europe itself. At the forefront of all platform builders' minds is the thought that unless they develop existing expertise in electronics or acquire it through vertical integration, the growth of electronics in weapons systems may relegate them to the position of sub-contractor in future.

For the biggest companies there are the further options of surviving through diversification outside defence or losing identity through mergers with larger industrial conglomerates less dependent on defence. Ferranti's forced sale of its defence division to GEC early in 1990 is unlikely to mark the end of a spiralling process of industrial rationalization of this kind.

The scale on which such development will happen depends on three factors. First, the extent to which, in the electronics field, where civil and military applications of technology are peculiarly intertwined, rationalization will be hampered by a wish to preserve national autonomy and/or national competition. Secondly, whether there is the political will to deliver as well as promise an open pan-European defence market. Thirdly, progress in East–West arms reductions. If a CFE treaty or treaties and the events of autumn 1989 lead to US force reductions from Europe, there will be an associated pressure to maintain national industrial capabilities. These will, however, be reduced from current levels as Europe takes its own 'peace dividend' and smaller defence budgets shrink the European market

Much of the concentration that has been seen so far in Europe has been confined within national borders. The absorption of MBB by Daimler-Benz, and Aérospatiale and Thomson CSF's merger of their aerospace electronics interests to form a joint subsidiary, Sextant Avionique, with a turnover of $600 m, making it Europe's largest defence avionics supplier,[8] are cases in point. Italy has also set about creating a rationalized defence base. IRI, the Institute for Industrial Reconstruction, has been reformed to establish two specialized groups, one concerned with high-tech and defence and the other with telecommunications.[9] And the state-owned and -run French army weapons producer GIAT is reportedly to be hived off to enable it to form joint ventures.[10] However, there have as yet been very few large-scale cross-border acquisitions within the European defence industries, although there have been many alliances. But the GEC/Siemens acquisition of Plessey, and Thompson CSF's acquisition of Philips Defence Industries could mark a sea-change.

In continental Europe, state control of the process of industrialization was, in the 19th century, one of the means by which governments created the states they notionally governed. Hence protectionism in industry, particularly the defence industry, which it was convenient to regard as lying close to the heart of statehood, is more deeply rooted in mainland Europe than in the UK. This makes the UK defence industry vulnerable to foreign predators. Mrs Thatcher's is the only EEC government whose rhetoric even contemplates the break-up and sale of a 'flag-carrier' firm.[11] Elsewhere in Europe it is basically a question of how long the cost of preserving national flag-carrying dinosaurs from extinction can be borne. The ubiquitous, but wholly inappropriate sporting metaphor of the 'unlevel playing field', used to describe competition policy in Europe, is valid. National industrial policies are hindering European economies from restructuring to meet competition from the US and the Far East, particularly in defence (although, in the defence field, serious competition from Far East industries is not yet imminent).

The EC Commissioner responsible for competition would no doubt also add, somewhat ambivalently, that there are dangers both in creating and preserving national monopolies (which rarely become world beaters), and in supporting the creation of giant pan-European firms which stifle competition. As always, it is a question of where the balance needs to be struck. For the present the most significant determinant is that, as Table 4 (p. 40) shows, major defence firms in France are state-owned, which prevents them being acquired, while in Germany they are largely owned by the banks.

That is not the only handicap to structural realignment throughout Europe. The importance of keeping on the right side of the Americans, preserving such access as Europe has to their markets and not making them feel industrially threatened has already been discussed, as has the long-term nature of defence contracts. A further factor is that national needs for highly classified 'black' contracts, especially in the growing electronics sector, will always mean that some national capacity has to be retained, and politicians' enthusiasm for clutching at whatever rationale the industrial lobby gives them for national preference can be expected to remain as strong as ever. Nonetheless, there are no fundamental reasons which prevent the creation of pan-European competing consortia, consortia with US membership, or even multinational European defence companies.

The eventual size, shape and make-up of these alliances or corporations will be a function of a complex set of interrelationships between technical demands, industrial resources and government policies towards national DIBs. Although the developments that have been described are likely to be large scale, movement of big pieces on the international defence industries' chessboard will not be continuous. There will be pauses during which managements and shareholders consolidate their gains and take stock of their position. Moreover, as has been noted, large projects take many years to set up and complete. During this period procurement systems and industrial relationships tend to ossify. At such times the greatest scope for introducing increased competition may lie in the myriad of lower value contracts which, typically, account for more than half of the equipment expenditure of the countries discussed in this Paper.

The events of 1989
It is difficult to assess whether the conclusions to be reached on the basis of this analysis are altered fundamentally by the dramatic changes in the Soviet Union and the political map of Europe, which occurred during 1989. These, taken together with an initial round of CFE negotiations likely to leave five categories of NATO's equipment holdings 5–10% below current levels, (to say nothing of the possibility of much deeper negotiated cuts in a second round), make it all too possible that the political consensus which currently sustains high levels of defence spending in the US and some European countries will evaporate rapidly, leading to massive and perhaps unilateral expenditure cuts in the short term. Despite the present 'business as usual' posture which predominates, cuts are inevitable: it is only a question of how much and how soon.

Events may show that the effect of the forthcoming reductions on defence suppliers as a whole has been exaggerated. Their survival strategy, which has led to rapid diversification and concentration, has already described, and the largest and fittest firms on the one hand and the niche market specialists on the other are likely to remain in being, particularly if they forge transnational links. Moreover, governments are all too conscious of the social and economic cost, not to speak of the practical difficulties, of large-scale attempts to turn tanks into tractors. They might therefore be tempted to argue the case for 'keeping up our guard', whether the need is real or not. As further evidence, it is noteworthy that the share price of 20 leading UK defence companies fell 19.4% between July and December 1989, when the market as a whole was rising.[12] Since stock markets are notoriously prone to overreaction, this may be as good an indication as any that the effects might not be as bad as first thought, at least as far as national purchases are concerned.

The prospects for export sales between Alliance countries look bleaker, notably because of the ministerial agreement that CFE reductions will lead to old equipment being scrapped and the newer shared out in an arrangement which will benefit the poorer nations. The NATO reduction of 2,200 main battle tanks currently envisaged will, for example, provide considerable potential for second-hand modern tanks being used to re-equip some nations with older fleets, who might in due course have been obliged to buy new weapons.

The results of this seem likely to be twofold. First, firms will have to redouble their efforts to compete in shrinking non-Alliance export markets. Coupled with this, US firms will be obliged to try to sell harder in Europe, though European governments will be acutely aware of the political sensitivity of both cutting defence spending and then spending the reduced budget abroad. This points to the events of 1989 tending to increase the pressure for US firms to join international consortia. Secondly, companies in countries where governments have been prepared to buy abroad will want to try to reverse the policy. Will they be successful? It would be foolish to generalize. Decisions will continue to be taken on a case-by-case basis. But such straws in the wind as there are, for example the UK's preparedness to accept and even foster GEC's acquisition of Ferranti, leaving only one national contractor capable, alone, of developing advanced airborne radars suggests that if new equipment is wanted governments will have no alternative but to seek to keep prices down through fully internationalizing competition, rather than buying exclusively from national industries, a protected European market, or continuing to engage in artificially structured collaboration. There is thus at least some prospect that smaller equipment budgets will in themselves promote greater efficiency in defence procurement.

CONCLUSIONS

There is nothing remarkable about the arguments in this Paper, which point to the need for change in the way in which the defence industries are structured and Western European governments buy their equipment. Indeed, its central proposition is that budgetary pressures, coupled with arms reduction developments, will in any case force changes: it is only a matter of determining the best way to go for the future.

Attitudes have already altered, even if action has yet to follow. In 1985, Sir Frank Cooper, who had been the top official in the UK MOD, cited a formidable list of constraints on progress, ranging from political difficulty, through loss of sovereignty, jobs, technology and exports, to the creation of another European bureaucracy. His argument was that it had not been demonstrated that the benefits of a common market would outweigh its costs, and that even if it did have a net benefit, the difficulties of bringing it into being had been underestimated. What was needed was for European governments to commission a study which would 'determine how best to create and shape the future.'[1] By the following year Vredeling had started work.

The deficiencies of the IEPG's Action Plan, of which Vredeling was the progenitor, leave no doubt that Cooper's judgement that defence ministers would find the political price of major reform too high, was sound. Nonetheless, the Action Plan represents progress of a sort. Moreover, despite the rhetoric that is usually employed to maintain its value, the political price of the fundamental change called for here may not be as high as many fear. As things are, sustained by industrialists suggesting that 'radical changes can only be achieved through strong political commitments'[2] and 'unpopular political decisions will be involved',[3] policy-makers tend to conclude that there are far too many existing sources of discontent within Europe to make the risks and gains from putting another on the agenda worthwhile. Even academics engage in extraordinary contortions to preserve the *status quo*. Thus, it would have been 'politically unacceptable to have seriously considered a foreign submarine-builder for Britain's nuclear deterrent'[4] despite the American origin of its missile system. Alternatively, 'it would no doubt be unwise to advocate a systematic opening of national defence procurement to international bidding.'[5] Quite why this is necessarily the case is never explained, but the comments are indicative and they allow and even encourage governments to overplay the sovereignty card, the political value of which could fall quite sharply if the present demand for a peace dividend becomes a clamour.

As it is, in the defence industries, national champions, who have gone the way of the dodo in many other sectors of the US and European economies, contine to be protected and promoted – an arrangement in which the firms themselves not surprisingly connive. The motive for the order-givers is not solely the preservation of sovereignty. For the Europeans there are real and genuine fears of the consequences of unnecessary dependence on the US. However, whilst in many manufacturing sectors 'national champion' policies are now untenable because companies have to compete on a global scale, there is as yet no global defence market: indeed, there is no European one. Even so, with the growth of dual-use technologies it makes decreasing sense to treat a company's defence business differently from its civil business. Moreover, meddling with market mechanisms is not only expensive but in the long run tends to make the companies in the market internationally uncompetitive.

If shortage of money is making such a policy unaffordable and defence markets are already in transition, who should manage the change and what should be the outcome? In Europe, the first question appears to have been settled with the adoption of the IEPG's Action Plan. However, the weaknesses in the plan mean that, even in the unlikely event of its full and rapid implementation, it will not revolutionize European procurement. The most important contribution that the IEPG can make is to direct its energies to the work of harmonizing requirements – forcing through the compromises which are the stuff of progress. Any role that it might play in creating and regulating competition should be delayed until there is sound evidence of political willingness, by all the governments concerned, to accept a policy of competition. But competition will only be accepted as the preferred policy if its virtues are assessed fairly alongside those of the alternative options. As far as the future make-up of the defence industries and the procurement policies which will shape them are concerned, the choices lie between:

a) collaboration along established lines with *juste retour* as the underlying principle;
b) systematic and progressive opening of markets to competition, but with deregulation remaining partial even outside nuclear and 'black' areas;
c) leaving to one side national 'black' contracts, creating a free market in which the demands of technology and cost oblige firms to co-operate.

Collaboration
The first question to be answered is whether, if markets are to be distorted by *juste retour*, nations should artificially preserve competition *within* their own country? The answer emerging from this examination of the procurement scene is that if market forces genuinely allow more than one national firm to survive, the competition thus engendered is all to the good, but there are no longer enough orders to go round to make the *artificial* preservation of competition affordable. As for the wider question, the die has already been cast. *Juste retour* is central to the Action Plan, even though in theory the return is to be spread across projects. It requires a considerable act of faith to believe that is what

will happen. Nations will want their *retour* in the bank rather than in vague promises of future recompense.

Supporters of collaboration in high technology sometimes argue that although they recognize it as second best to the abolition of internal market barriers, it is only a transitional stage. Firms pool R&D resources and collectively spend more, thereby enabling them to become in due time more competitive. However, it is not obvious how today's collaborators can become tomorrow's competitors. Moreover, collaboration based on *juste retour* does not sharpen competitiveness, nor does it lead to the formation of the competing transnational European consortia which the IEPG advocates. In fact, sticking to the principle of *juste retour* while simultaneously trying to introduce competition leads to bizarre outcomes when nations have only one company in a given industrial sector. If *juste retour* demands that each nation is represented in each consortium, the national company cannot lose, whoever wins the contract. This is the happy position in which FIAR in Italy and INISEL in Spain find themselves in the contest for EFA radar. And even if this were not the case, the work-sharing arrangements which underpin *juste retour* could mean that the 'winning' firm would be obliged to sub-contract work to the 'losers'. Peculiarities of this kind are inherent in the way in which collaboration is currently organized. Even though its economic efficiency has been raised by governments insisting on the maximum amount of competition for equipment and sub-systems, the inefficiencies of present models of collaboration in platform manufacture, particularly their lack of shared objectives and firm direction, outweigh any technological strengthening and development they might generate.

Limited competition
Those who accept this conclusion often persuade themselves that it is unrealistic to expect things to change, and that, since something is better than nothing, a political decision to open individual categories of equipment, components, parts or sub-assemblies to competition, either within Europe or internationally, with the IEPG ensuring fair play, is the thing to do. This would indeed be a welcome extension of the competitive bidding currently used at sub-contract level in collaborative programmes. There is no doubt that it is feasible and that it would be beneficial. It would also be possible to cover a significant proportion of equipment purchases. However, cost savings are likely to be proportionately greatest on low value items. Experience of competitive tendering on high value items suggests that suppliers will work with the grain of national preference by sharing work with local partners, thereby increasing costs. In many instances the international consortia bids for EFA's equipment were higher than those from sole national suppliers. And, in a field tending to be dominated by caution and a preference for maintaining the *status quo*, par-

tial deregulation will not necessarily provide any incentive to move progressively towards a fully open market. Defence procurement may simply get stuck in a different groove.

The free market

The question then remains, how much longer can the gains from fully open competition in driving costs down and stimulating creativity be foregone? Are the unique features of defence contracting, with a single customer dictating the product and able to alter the market size at will – factors which tend to lead to monopolies – sufficient to make a free international market unthinkable?

There is a risk that the removal of subsidy and protection in such a specialized area, without controls on mergers and acquisitions, will eliminate competition and lead to US domination of Europe, or domination within Europe by one country's industrial giant. This is obviously undesirable, but the cost of not taking those risks has now become too high.

In the event, a switch to a free market is unlikely to have the dire consequences that some predict. When civil markets open, as the rash of acquisitions in Europe shows, the natural economic response is to buy and merge rather than collaborate. Joint ventures are designed to gain market access where trade barriers exist. However, even if defence markets are opened, defence manufacturers, selling in an environment of long-established and deeply-entrenched national preference are likely to find it better to team together rather than buy one another out. Moreover, although takeovers cannot be ruled out, European governments will not immediately privatize their state-owned firms so that they can be bought, or allow important privately owned contractors to pass into overseas ownership, although there will be in-country mergers and acquisitions. On the other hand, it will not be possible to hold out against large foreign shareholdings. And if restructuring did reach the point where foreign acquisition was tolerated, with proper safeguards, there need not necessarily be any loss of identity or national capability. French companies now own a significant number of the UK's water supply undertakings. This development does not seem to have caused international incidents.

The most significant change from the present situation therefore would be that, while the IEPG busied itself with the task of harmonizing and simplifying requirements, industry would be left free to restructure itself through whatever forms of co-operation market forces dictate. It is the legislative and political freedom for industry to determine its own future which is important. Governments cannot do better than firms in identifying factors for successful co-operation.

DIBs, whether national or international, will not be made leaner overnight. Progress will most easily be made through teaming to bid competitively against specific requirements. Compatible partners will not necessarily be found first time round. But, in time, the transnational consortia favoured by the IEPG should emerge. Governments would no longer need to put together new groupings for each project. It might even lead to the eventual realization of the long-standing dream of specialization in national manufacturing, because placing orders with a single international company, leaving the work to be distributed in the most economical manner, will tend to promote a concentration of national expertise. Such a development would allow reciprocal purchasing on the lines now being pioneered by France and the UK to flourish, and encourage a greater willingness to buy 'off-the-shelf' from abroad.

Naturally there are penalties involved. Industrial rationalization cannot be bloodless at any time, and it cannot but be more painful at a time of shrinking demand. Employment in the defence industries would fall, only the fittest firms would survive, and any aspirations of the LDDI nations to establish large-scale manufacturing capabilities across a broad spectrum would not be met. Unhealthily large firms might emerge. Co-operation between public and private sector companies would be difficult to organize fairly. International relations could be strained. European industry would not necessarily be strengthened as much as expected because the transatlantic links that were formed might prove stronger than the inter-European ones. By definition, competition does not please everybody. Nonetheless, those industrial companies which are competitive, *are* anxious to start the process, and nations cannot afford the time or money needed for the others to catch up. Nor is it at all self-evident that 'closer collaboration will demand a hitherto undreamt-of exercise of political will.'[6]

In an Adelphi Paper written 20 years ago, Geoffrey Ashcroft noted that 'the concept of fair shares and equality of treatment has become established as a, if not the, cardinal principle of European collaboration'.[7] It still is. It is time it was dislodged.

Notes

Introduction

[1] *The European Defence Dossier*, vol. 1 (Southampton: BDMI Ltd, 1989), p. 8.

[2] Fifth Report from the House of Commons Defence Committee of Session 1987–88, *The Procurement of Major Defence Equipment* (London: Her Majesty's Stationery Office, 1988), p.v.

[3] Roger Facer, *The Alliance and Europe: Part III, Weapons Procurement in Europe – Capabilities and Choices*, Adelphi Paper 108, Winter 1974, p. 8.

[4] Edward Heath, 'Why Opt Out of the Future?' *The Guardian*, 13 October 1989.

[5] *Proceedings of a Colloquy on European Cooperation in Armaments Research and Development* (London: Western European Union, 1988), p. 27.

[6] Government Response to the Fifth Report from the House of Commons Defence Committee of Session 1987–8, *The Procurement of Major Defence Equipment* (London: Her Majesty's Stationery Office, 1988), para. 20.

[7] *Proceedings*, (*op. cit.* in note 5), p. 19.

[8] *Jane's NATO and Europe Today*, 19 April 1989, p. 3.

[9] *Jane's NATO Report*, 15 November 1988, p. 1.

[10] 1989 Mintel Special Report – British Lifestyle 1988, *The Guardian*, 26 January 1989.

[11] Trevor Taylor, *Defence Technology and International Integration* (London: Francis Pinter, 1982), p. 191.

Chapter 1

[1] *Statement on the Defence Estimates 1988*, vol. 2 CMD 344–11 (London: Her Majesty's Stationery Office, 1988), p. 17.

[2] NATO Defence Planning Committee, *Enhancing Alliance Collective Security – Shared Roles, Risks and Responsibilities in the Alliance* (Brussels: NATO, 1988), p. 68.

[3] *Ibid*, p. 32.

[4] *IEPG Action Plan*, para. 2.2.

[5] *Ministerial Communique* (IEPG/MIN/D11: Luxembourg), 9 November 1988.

[6] Article 223 of the Treaty of Rome reads:
1. The provisions of this Treaty shall not prevent the following rules from applying:

(a) No member State shall be obliged to supply information the disclosure of which it considers contrary to the essential interests of its security;
(b) Any Member State may take whatever measures it considers necessary for the protection of the essential interests of its security and which are connected with the production of or trade in arms, munitions and war material; such measures shall, however, not adversely affect conditions of competition in the common market regarding products which are not intended for specifically military purposes.
2. During the first year after this Treaty comes into force, the Council shall, by unanimous decision, determine the lists of products to which the provisions of paragraph 1 (b) shall apply.
3. The Council may, by unanimous decision, on a proposal from the Commission, amend this list.

[7] *COM(88) 376 FINAL 11-10-88*, para. 372.

[8] 'Community Plan for Arms Tariff', *The Independent*, 18 May 1988; 'Protests Bog Down European Import Tariff on US Defense Goods', *Defense News*, 30 January 1989.

[9] Personal interviews.

[10] *Jane's NATO Report*, (*op. cit.* in Introduction, note 9), p. 5.

Chapter 2

[1] *The European Defence Dossier*, (*op. cit.* in Introduction, note 1), p. 7.

[2] *Ibid*, p. 7.

[3] Unpublished UK Ministry of Defence estimates.

[4] Jacques Gansler, *The Defence Industry* (London: The MIT Press, 1980).

[5] UBS Phillips & Drew, *Pan European Electronics Review* (London: UBS Phillips & Drew, 1989), p. 9.

[6] Terrell G. Covington, Keith W. Brendley, Mary E. Chenoweth, *A Review of European Arms Collaboration and Prospects for its Expansion* (Santa Monica CA: RAND Corporation, 1987), p. 11.

[7] Hoare Govett, *Electronics Monthly* (London: Hoare Govett Investment Research Ltd., 1989), p. iv.

8 *Ibid*, p.v.
9 *The Times*, 19 November 1989.
10 *Electronics Monthly*, (*op. cit.* in note 7), p. iii.
11 Hoare Govett, *European Defence: Winds of Change* (London: Hoare Govett Investment Research Ltd., 1988), p. 13.
12 *Ibid.*, pp. 18–37.
13 *Business Week*, 8 January 1990.
14 The definitional problems involved can be shown by comparing NATO's equipment percentage figure for the UK in 1988 (24.7%) with the UK government's figure of 43% given in the Fifth Report from the House of Commons Defence Committee of Session 1987–88 (*op. cit.* in Introduction, note 2).
15 *The Implication of the European Community's 1992 Programme for US Industry* (Unpublished paper by the US Department of Commerce, International Trade Administration Division, 1989).
16 US Arms Control and Disarmament Agency, *World Military Expenditures and Arms Transfers 1987* (Washington DC: 1988), p. 10.
17 *Pan European Electronics Review*, (*op. cit.* in note 5), pp. 4–6.
18 Gansler, (*op. cit.* in note 4), p. 257.
19 The Centre for Strategic and International Studies, *Deterrence in Decay: The Future of the US Defense Industrial Base* (Washington DC: 1989), p. 32.
20 Keith Hartley, 'The European Defence Market and Industry', in Pauline Creasey and Simon May (eds.), *The European Armaments Market and Procurement Cooperation* (London: The Macmillan Press Ltd., 1988), p. 48.
21 Ministère de la Défense, *The French Defence Industry* (Paris: 1988), p. 26.
22 *Ibid.*, p. 7.
23 *Ibid.*, p. 14 and *Statement on the Defence Estimates 1988*, (*op. cit.* in Chapter 1, note 1), p. 61.
24 *The Economist*, 15 April 1989, p. 34.
25 *Ibid.*
26 'France's Defence Procurement "Must Go High-Tech"', *Financial Times*, 12 March 1990.
27 *The European Defence Dossier*, (*op. cit.*, in Introduction, note 1), p. 7.
28 *European Defence: Winds of Change*, (*op. cit.*, in note 11), p. 28.

29 Federal Ministry of Defence, *The Situation and Development of the Federal Armed Forces* (Bonn: 1985).
30 *Statement on the Defence Estimates 1988*, (*op. cit.* in Chapter 1, note 1), p. 61.
31 *Ibid.*, p. 15.
32 In a report published in 1985 the UK's Comptroller and Auditor General put the figure at one-third. *Ministry of Defence Collaborative Projects* HCP 626 (London: Her Majesty's Stationery Office, 1985).
33 Unpublished report for the Department of Trade and Industry (DTI).
34 *European Defence: Winds of Change* (*op. cit.* in note 11).
35 NEDO, *Performance and Competitive Success: Strengthening Competitiveness in UK Electronics* (London: 1988), p. 9.
36 Keith Hartley, Farooq Hussain, Ron Smith, *The Political Quarterly*, vol. 58, no. 1 (Oxford: Basil Blackwell Ltd., 1987), p. 72.
37 *Hansard*, Col. 116, 18 December 1986.
38 *Statement on the Defence Estimates 1988*, (*op. cit.* in Chapter 1, note 1), p. 13 and Trevor Taylor and Keith Hayward, *The UK Defence Industrial Base: Development and Future Policy Options* (London: Brassey's, 1989), p. 34.
39 Unpublished DTI report, (*op. cit.* in note 33).
40 Robert C. McCormack, 'Bolstering Defence Industrial Competitiveness through International Cooperation', *Defence Issues*, vol. 3, no. 50, p. 12.

Chapter 3

1 *Deterrence in Decay*, (*op. cit.* in Chapter 2, note 19), p. 3.
2 Unpublished DTI report, (*op. cit.* in Chapter 2, note 33), p. 100.
3 Ron Smith and Jacques Fontanel, 'Weapons Procurement: Domestic Production versus Imports' in Ian Bellany and Tim Huxley (eds.), *New Conventional Weapons and Western Defence*, (London: Frank Cass, 1987), p. 81.
4 Facer, (*op. cit.* in Introduction, note 3), p. 34.
5 See, for example, N. Kay, J.P. Robe, and P. Lagnoli, *An Approach to the Analysis of Joint Ventures* (European University Working Paper, 1987).
6 'Labour National Executive Committee Defence Proposals', *The Guardian*, 8 May 1989.

7 *Deterrence in Decay*, (*op. cit.* in Chapter 2, note 19), p. 37.

8 *Financial Times*, 8 November 1989.

9 Keith Hartley, 'Defence Procurement and Industrial Policy' in John Roper (ed.), *The Future of British Defence Policy* (Aldershot: Gower, 1985), p. 180.

10 Keith Hartley, NATO Advisory Group for Aerospace Research and Development, Conference Proceedings, No 424, 1988, pp. 947–53.

11 *Ibid.*, p. 925.

12 Fifth Report, (*op. cit.* in Introduction, note 2), p. xviii.

13 Market Access International Ltd., *The Politics of British Defence Procurement* (London: 1989), p. 141.

14 'Euro-Fighter Hopes Take a Dive', *Sunday Telegraph,* 18 March 1990.

15 Keith Hartley, 'Defence Industrial Policy' in G. Hall (ed.), *European Industrial Policy* (London: Croom Helm, 1986), p. 255.

16 'Frigate Options Narrow as Navies Back NATO Plan', *Financial Times*, 11 October 1989.

17 *Towards a Stronger Europe* (Brussels: IEPG, 1987), vol. 2, p. 120.

18 Fifth Report, (*op. cit.* in Introduction, note 2), p. xxvi.

19 David Perry and Giuseppe Piavano, 'EH101 – An Innovative Approach to Collaboration', *NATO's Sixteen Nations*, no. 6, 1985, p. 75.

20 'Helicopter Jobs at Risk Over Cut in Investment', *Daily Telegraph*, 13 November 1989.

21 Comptroller and Auditor General (*op. cit.* in Chapter 2, note 32), p. 7.

22 Seventh Report from the House of Commons Defence Committee of Session 1987–8, *The Defence Estimates* HCP 495 (London: Her Majesty's Stationery Office, 1988), p. xv.

23 *Ibid.*, p. 35.

24 J. Moray Stewart, 'Defence Procurement in Britain', *RUSI Journal*, Winter 1988, p. 45.

25 Personal interview.

26 Personal interview.

Chapter 4

1 Creasey and May (*op. cit.* in Chapter 2, note 20), p. 75.

2 Margaret Sharp and Christine Shearman, *European Technological Collaboration* (London: Routledge, 1987), p. 113.

3 'Guide to Europe's Collaborative Research Programmes', *Financial Times*, 22 March 1989.

4 *Jane's NATO and Europe Today*, 4 July 1989, p. 1.

5 *Ibid.*

6 Euromart, *European Strategic Programme for Aeronautical Research and Technology* (Brussels: European Aeronautics Industries, 1989).

7 *The Guardian*, 16 January 1990.

8 *Defense News*, 5 December 1988.

9 *Ibid.*

10 *Financial Times*, 15 January 1990.

11 *The Economist*, 14 January 1989, p. 23.

12 BBC TV *Newsnight*, 24 January 1990.

Conclusions

1 Frank Cooper, *Preconditions for the Emergence of a European Common Market in Armaments* (Brussels: CEPS Papers no. 18, 1985), p. 25.

2 Raymond Lygo, *Future Challenges to the European Defence Industrial Base* (Brussels: European Defence Industry Study Group, 1989), para. 8.

3 *Proceedings*, (*op. cit.* in Introduction, note 5), p. 51.

4 Taylor and Hayward, (*op. cit.* in Chapter 2, note 38), p. 131.

5 Creasey and May (*op. cit.* in Chapter 2, note 20), p. 173.

6 *Proceedings*, (*op. cit.* in Introduction, note 5), p. 56.

7 Geoffrey Ashcroft, *Military Logistic Systems in NATO: The Goal of Integration. Part I – Economic Aspects*, Adelphi Paper 61, November 1969, p. 20.